"Peak Performance: Mindset Tools for Athletes *human spirit, tenacity, and meeting ourselves where we're at, in order to achieve our personal peak performance. I was captivated and brought into the personal worlds of each of the authors' stories, and I was made to think a little deeper about my personal lived experiences. What is my best? Could I go farther, higher, faster? Am I willing to dig deep enough to find those reserves of energy we all have but don't often access?* Peak Performance: Mindset Tools for Athletes *brings to life the human spirit and our desire to search for our deeper selves and push our limits... to the peak...whatever that peak may be for you.*"

—JENNIFER J. SAUNDERS, Righteous ReBEl
Adventures and Coaching, Play Advocate, Speaker

"Peak Performance: Mindset Tools for Athletes *is a resource for anyone involved in sport whatever your level. Each chapter highlights strategies that have proved successful and underpins these with evidence. I particularly enjoyed the anecdotes the authors reveal, and I now consider how I can apply them to both my professional and personal life. This book is reference source to which I am sure I will constantly refer.*"

—GARY ANDERSON, Olympic Medal Winning
Performance Director, Olympic Team Leader

"*To reach an elite level in sports today, it takes more than just talent. The top performers on the podium are now engineered for success.* Peak Performance: Mindset Tools for Athletes *looks at factors that increase performance beyond just working hard: such as focusing on what is in your control, becoming a student obsessed with learning every aspect of your sport, and learning to love the training as much as the competition. Each chapter stands alone as an easily digestible bite-size bit of wisdom but, taken all together, they create a feast of a book for anyone looking to be the very best version of themselves.*"

—DANIEL CHRISTOFFERSON, LMT,
Founder of Holistic High Performance LLC

"*Erik Seversen has successfully brought together another incredible group of experts whose personal experience and knowledge provide practical wisdom for all.* Peak Performance: Mindset Tools for Athletes *is a fantastic book for athletes and coaches. The tools found within each chapter can significantly benefit everyone who wants peak performance in their own life, whether an athlete or not. A common thread within the chapters is preparation. Preparation helps you push through adversity to succeed in sports, business, and life. Meal prep keeps an athlete adequately fueled. Mental preparation trains you to respond to challenges and take charge of your life rather than reacting and allowing emotion to take over. If you want to improve confidence, focus, and motivation and manifest success in your life, this book is for you!"*

—DENISE E. STEGALL, Founder and Curator of Living Healthy List, International Best-Selling Author

"When we think of athletes at the highest level, we immediately think of the physical preparation behind their successful achievements. In Peak Performance: Mindset Tools for Athletes, *we are taken on a journey of connecting the mind, body, and soul—where athletes perform at their best. In each of the chapters, the co-authors focus on different, and yet very essential, areas of importance that make the book an extraordinary toolbox for anyone who is on the path of becoming a peak performer or already is and wants to reach the next level of performance in their athletic life. The book serves as a guide for turning thoughts into action. This is a must-read for anyone seeking the secret recipes of success and Peak Performance."*

—SOHAIL MICHAEL PEDARI, Leadership Coach and Learning Specialist, Goalkeeper Coach

"If you read through Peak Performance: Mindset Tools for Athletes, *you will see that every top athlete has a strong moment of experience, which transformed their mindset in regard of self-belief, work ethic, goal setting, and perseverance from one with an average performance to become a peak achiever. Whether you are an athlete who is working to achieve a professional level of performance, a coach helping such an athlete, or a parent trying to help your child excel in sports, this book has the potential to transform your mindset to one of a peak achiever."*

—RIAD HECHAME, Nuclear Engineer, Performance Coach, Founder of Peak Human Performance

PEAK PERFORMANCE

PEAK PERFORMANCE

Mindset Tools for
ATHLETES

Authored by:
Erik Seversen, Logan Anderson, Luis Araya, David Arsenault, Norma Bastidas,
Emily Buckley, Tarek Charaf, PhD, Robert Fegg, Sacha Fulton, PhD, Ryne Glazier,
Jonathan Harris-Wright, Matt Helke, Bashir A. Ismail, Jennifer Kavanagh,
Kristin Kaye, Jen Yung Lee, Scott MacDonald, Kurt Madden, Akari Nakahara,
Solly Nowrozi, Maximus Redfield, Shari Reiniger, Jack Seversen, Kylie Tullipan,
Julia Catherine Vincent, Adam Whisler, Doron Willis

THIN LEAF PRESS | LOS ANGELES

Library of Congress Cataloging-in-Publication Data
Names: Seversen, Erik, Author, et al.
Title: *Peak Performance: Mindset Tools for Athletes*
LCCN: 2022919881

ISBN 978-1-953183-16-3 (hardcover) | 978-1-953183-17-0 (paperback)
ISBN 978-1-953183-18-7 (eBook) | 978-1-953183-19-4 (audiobook)
Sports Training, Athletic Coaching, Performance
Cover Design: 100 Covers
Interior Design: Formatted Books
Editor: Nancy Pile
Thin Leaf Press
Los Angeles

THIN
LEAF

Thank you for reading this book. There are tools found within the following pages that can greatly benefit your life, but don't stop there. Make sure you get the most you can from this book and reach out directly to the expert-authors who want to help you reach your goals by performing at peak levels as an athlete and to manifest success in your life. Contact information for each author is found at the end of their respective chapter.

To youth, college, Olympic, and professional athletes around the world who have put in the work and to the coaches who help them achieve the highest levels of performance and success.

CONTENTS

INTRODUCTION

By Erik Seversen
Author of *Ordinary to Extraordinary* and *Explore*
Los Angeles, California

I had a meeting with Olympic athlete, Fabian Florant last week to discuss the book, *The Successful Spirit*, we co-authored in 2021. Over fancy ginger-based exotic juice drinks at a swanky Beverly Hills café, Fabian told me how he'd try to psychologically intimidate his opponents in the triple jump. Fabian described how, when competing at international championships, he'd perform his first jump and then immediately take off his track shoes, even though each competitor was given three jump attempts for the competition. Fabian knew that his long triple jump, combined with his confidence that no other competitors would match it, would break their will. He knew that if they felt defeated at the start, they would be defeated. They would be limited by their own belief. This technique worked, and, at the time of this writing, Fabian Florant holds the record (16.92 meters) for the longest triple jump for a Dutch athlete.

Fabian's story is also a story that anything is possible. Born in the Caribbean, Fabian was a stand-out athlete in track, but he knew that to reach the highest levels of peak performance in his sport, he couldn't just work hard. He eventually outgrew the support that his country, Dominica, could provide and was accepted to compete for the Dutch National Team, which eventually led to Fabian's Olympic debut at the 2016 Summer Olympics in Rio de Janeiro.

I begin with Fabian's story because his story could be yours. While your sport might not be track and field and you might not have been born in

Dominica, our human condition is so similar that we can draw lessons from each other's experiences. We can learn from Fabian that anything is possible.

If you are an aspiring athlete or a coach intending to help your athletes go to the next level in their sport, it is time to take a deep breath and look at factors that increase performance beyond just working hard. The days of hard-work-equals-peak-performance are over. Sure, hard work is a major factor in athletic success for both individual and team sports, but, today, most top athletes and coaches would agree that it takes much, much more than that.

Today, things like resistance training, visualization, meditation, breathing techniques, support communities, performance-enhancing monitoring with new technologies, nutrition, and much more are involved in attaining peak performance in sports. In today's world, the mind, body, and spirit should act as one with both physical and mental components factoring into training regimens. If you are an athlete or coach hungry to reach higher levels in your sport, you are reading the right book. This book is a toolkit for you to select which tools are best for your particular situation.

Since I believe there are multiple routes to individual peak performance, I didn't try to write this book, *Peak Performance: Mindset Tools for Athletes*, by myself. Rather, I also solicited the help of 25 experts from various backgrounds and locations. Since there is no one-size-fits-all prescription for peak performance as an athlete, the experts in this book come with different perspectives. The experts and perspectives are from all over the USA, Canada, Scotland, Ireland, Greece, Norway, Qatar, and Australia. The areas of expertise include a wide spectrum from athletic excellence, academic study, sport nutrition, psychology, conditioning, coaching, refereeing, and more.

The authors of this book are professionals who are mindset and peak performance coaches, fitness and conditioning trainers, leadership, national team, and Olympic coaches, psychologists, PhDs, holistic performance coaches, gym owners, and nutritionists.

The athletes who helped author this book have competed professionally in individual and team sports and have won medals in Division I College, National Championships, Olympics, Paralympics, and more. These athletes have competed or coached in various sports including weightlifting, track and field, water polo, taekwondo, triathlon, marathon, CrossFit, luge, soccer, football, lacrosse, baseball, figure skating, sled hockey, squash, diving, and more.

As elite athletes and coaches, the authors in this book also include Olympic committee members, military combat veterans, Guinness World Record holders, hall of fame inductees, and more. The one thing these individuals have in common is that they all have a clear idea about peak performance, and these ideas can be applied to any situation in athletics and in life. These ideas are available to you now.

Although this book is organized around the united theme of mindset and peak performance for athletes, each chapter is totally stand-alone. The chapters in the book can be read in any order. I encourage you to look through the table of contents and begin wherever you want. However, I urge you to read all the chapters because, as a whole, they provide a great array of perspectives. Each is valuable in helping you tap into your full potential by adding peak performance strategies to your sport and life.

It is my hope that you discover something in this book that helps take your performance to the next level, so you can enthusiastically reach new heights as an athlete and rapidly reach your goals.

Email: Erik@ErikSeversen.com
Website: www.ErikSeversen.com

CHAPTER ONE

KEEPING YOUR PEAK PERFORMANCE RELATIVE

By Logan Anderson, BA, CPT, CIFT
Owner, All Strong Fitness, Adaptive Fitness Coach
Bettendorf, Iowa

*When someone is properly grounded in life, they shouldn't
have to look outside themselves for approval.*
—Epictetus

What first comes to your mind when you think of the word "performance"? Do you think of an athlete running across a field at high speeds, cutting gracefully and precisely to evade opponents? Or perhaps you imagine a high school student honing their mental prowess to complete a standardized test at the top of their class? What about peak performance? What if that same athlete running across the field in the first example shaved an admirable one second off of an already elite 40-yard dash time? How about the high school student who is now studying law at Harvard University? Did I mention this student completed their bar exam at the top of their class? It would be hard to argue that these examples of performance and peak performance would be anything short of achieving excellence. In fact, these examples show precisely the ideals that society creates when thinking about performing at a high level. Unfortunately, something is missing here.

Of course, winning a track and field sprint in a major race is a great example of performing at the highest level; and of course, completing the law bar exam on the first try shows the true capacity of a driven individual's mental capability. What is the issue then? Shouldn't we all strive for greatness? The problem with these two examples being the standard of peak performance is that they are showing peak performance in an absolute sense. These examples of peak performance are essentially the ceiling of what performing at the highest level can be for society.

When we think of high-caliber performance, we don't think of an average individual. We don't think about that individual optimizing performance in the scope of their life. Is the problem with our view on peak performance starting to become evident? How is someone who has average genetics both physically and mentally supposed to live up to preconceived ideas often tied to peak performance? What about someone who is at the lowest tier of physical ability and cognition? The simple answer is, their performance can't and shouldn't be judged according to society's notion of peak performance.

Some might try to compare themselves directly to top performers, trying to match their own peak performance to people who largely exude excellence. This is usually done subconsciously, despite the fact that top levels of performance might not be reasonable, much less achievable, for them. As individuals, we often are stuck on the idea that maximizing performance is as rigid as a piece of steel, with no room for objectivity. Naturally, we cling to individuals who are already elite. We want to be just like them, not understanding the steps it takes to reach that type of performance. Our mindset is focused on how people at the top are excelling, instead of what we personally can do to excel.

So, what does that leave for most of us? What does that leave for the average man or woman who works an office job, enjoys the company of their friends at baseball games, and cherishes tucking in their kids before heading to bed? How about someone who steers even closer to the end of the "average" spectrum? Consider this—these individuals look at the elite performers and already start comparing themselves. "I'll never reach that level," they say, slowly defeating themselves before they even start.

With this mindset, why would someone who is average even bother? When looking at average individuals it may seem that peak performance might not matter for them. They are average for a reason, right? When looking at what average means, it is simply a way to classify and compare different things in life. Being average is a label. It is an identity people stick to because it is comfortable, and for many, it makes sense.

Thinking that someone who is average should not try to perform better, simply because they will never compare to high performers, is an incredibly narrow view of the world. Just think, can someone who is currently average at a given physical or mental task perform better at it? Yes. Can someone who is currently below average, reach the average level? You get the point.

Just because you may consider yourself an average performer now, doesn't always mean you have to stay there. As living and breathing humans, we have the ability to adapt physically, mentally, and emotionally. All it takes to perform at your highest level is being able to think you can. Once you switch your mindset inwards, you start to pave the road to performing at your highest potential. Should the average person just give up, succumbing to the ideals that society has put on them, encasing them in the "average" bubble? Of course not. The most crucial aspect of peak performance is making sure you look at it from a relative sense. Performing at your best should not be looked at through the same frame as that of the upper one percent in the world. Doing this causes envy and frustration, and skews what you think you should be able to accomplish for yourself. Objectively looking at where you are now, and where you and only you could get to, is the only way to truly perform at your highest level.

A short introduction, we have considered that our current views on performance and achieving progress might not be favorable for individuals themselves. Their idea of peak performance likely does not lie within. Often what we view as high performance is built off of what society has shaped our ideas to be.

With the example of the seemingly average person with an average life, we can begin to question the framework of how we view performing, not just well, but at our highest potential. Drawing a hard line between the top performers in society, with individuals that are considered average and even below average, gives just a glimpse of what kind of pressure society brings to the table. A very skewed view of performance, the notion that you need to be grinding out 12-plus hour days at the office, or training four-plus hours a day to reach your athletic prowess, is a view that, once challenged, can liberate you from the anxiety of comparing your performance to standards the outside world has developed.

Remember the example of the Harvard student passing the bar exam on their first try or the elite athlete decreasing their 40-yard dash time by a few seconds? Let's now compare these examples to the complete opposite spectrum of a population. Let's compare these examples to some individuals that by societal standards are performing at a very low level.

Imagine a 90-year-old man with two hip replacements, one knee replacement, and three back surgeries, struggling to get out of his favorite leather recliner at home. How does this example make you feel?

Now imagine an individual with Down syndrome, moderate intellectual disabilities, and a speech impediment trying to sound out his mother's name without stuttering.

What about a postpartum mother who is struggling trying to deal with the physical byproduct of delivering triplets?

Do any of these examples scream "performance," let alone "peak performance"?

The fact of the matter is that all of the individuals in these examples are exuding a level of performance, currently at their ability level. They don't seem quite as impressive as the individual sprinting across the playing field, or the high school student getting ready to take on the mental gauntlet of the ACT. The examples don't seem impressive, not because they aren't, but because our current views of peak performance are based on individuals working at a superhuman level. In reality, the examples are equal when looking through the peak performance lens relatively.

Of course, everyone can participate in a variety of activities, performing within their given capability level at the time. But what can the individuals in the most recent example truly improve on? What does peak performance look like to them? The answer lies in the fact that increasing their performance in life will look much different than the elite athlete or the recent Harvard graduate. The reason why the 90-year-old man, the individual with Down syndrome, or the postpartum mother seems less than the athlete and graduate is because of our comparison of them to the elite athlete and law student to begin with.

These two drastically different population sets should not be compared because their levels of current performance are not equal; thus, it's not a reliable way to measure relative success. Instead, let's look at how the elderly man, the individual with a disability, and the mother can mold peak performance goals for themselves. To do this, we need to look at what performance truly looks like for the individual, and not what society has skewed top performance to look like.

First, think about the 90-year-old man. Reaching peak performance for him might involve being able to independently get up off the ground for the first time in 20 years. This is incredibly impressive, but just the start.

How about the individual with varying physical and cognitive abilities? For the individual with Down syndrome, peak performance could entail winning an adaptive spelling bee for individuals with speech impairments and disabilities. Seems like these individuals who are "below average" are performing at a peak level, no?

What about the fatigued and defeated mother? Peak performance for her might look like finishing a 5-kilometer jog for the first time ever. I forgot to mention that she did this just months after giving birth to triplets, sustaining the mental and physical burden of caring for three living and breathing humans.

When the idea of performing at their best is curtailed for each respective individual, we can see how glorious they all are in their own personal triumphs. We can see how they grew to not just perform, but push their performance to their highest level. These examples are not based on what society deems as peak performance. These examples provide a personal and specific glimpse into what is important for that individual and how they pushed the boundaries for themselves.

As we can see, the whole idea comes down to increasing your performance in a relative manner. This is easier said than done, as most of our internal drive comes from some type of influence from the outside world. Society leads us in a direction, so that most of us consider our individual peak performance should equal that of becoming the best of the best. Being the richest in the nation, breaking the 100-meter dash at the Olympics, or public speaking to the masses at a high level are all examples that bleed into our thoughts when trying to make a performance goal for ourselves. As mentioned, comparing your performance to these feats is a waste of time because they don't address your life specifically.

I have worked with numerous individuals of varying abilities. Some have memory issues while others have physical and intellectual disabilities. These individuals don't struggle making performance goals relative. In fact, these individuals make large improvements into what they can achieve and perform. What makes them different? The common denominator for all of these individuals, compared to the general population, is that their ideas of peak performance all come from within.

An elderly lady I used to train had an extremely weak leg due to various surgeries. Many of the workouts that we did involved single-leg strengthening and stability exercises to improve this discrepancy. These workouts likely looked much different from the ones she did when she was younger. In addition, the workouts even looked different as compared to those of others her same age. Do you know what she thought about this? Absolutely nothing.

For individuals with disabilities, they stopped caring about what others think about their performance a long time ago. This individual cared only about one thing: reaching peak performance for herself. Through the subsequent months, this individual noticed something different when she got up onto the bus that transported her around the city. She said to me in an exuberant tone, "I can get up the bus stairs much easier now!" That is peak performance. Not what you used to be able to do. Not what others can do. But what you can do for yourself today that can make you better tomorrow.

A good place to start is to ask yourself this simple question: if you compare your performance to nobody else in the world, including yourself from the past, what does reaching peak performance look like for you? Pegging your mind with this question does two distinct things. It takes the comparison from individuals that are not you out of the question. This brings your mindset one step closer towards keeping performance within your own realm.

But we can't stop just there. The other aspect that this question addresses is your inner comparison. Making your performance goal relative is just as much about not comparing yourself to others, in addition to not comparing yourself today to your previous self. As you move through life, your body changes, your ideas of the world evolve, and your priorities mold into new and uncharted territories. Because of this, it is only natural that your ideas on performance in life flow naturally into these uncharted territories as well. If you start to let external influences in the world and society shape your performance goals, it is no longer relative.

Keeping yourself in check and realizing that your ideas on performance are straying from what is important for you, keeps your performance in physical, mental, and emotional pursuits in life strictly about what matters: your own personal development. Doing this offers a myriad of positive influences on your life. One of the most profound and meaningful influences that keeping your performance goals relative does is ease the frustration of not achieving something. At the end of the day, we only have so much mental, physical, and emotional energy to pour into our working and leisure lives. Trying to reach a level of performance not within our means can lead to burnout, in addition to the anxiety from not achieving what we tried so hard to accomplish. Balancing your life into the right amount of performing to resting is truly an art, and it is crucial to long-term success. With a mind open to change, you can start to make your thoughts on performance realistic and, in turn, work for you, not against you.

To close, I'll offer a point to ponder over. Profound, precisely timed questions can often steer our thoughts and actions in the right direction, moving us forward in life. Today, and in the days ahead, ask yourself, "How have societal views influenced my own personal view on increasing my performance?" Likely, society has influenced your entire view on increasing your performance in life and beyond.

Once you've considered this, you can also ask, "What is one small way I can change this view to be more relative for my life?" Keeping these questions handy and relating to them frequently will help keep your ideas of peak performance internal and entirely independent of society's harsh, critical, and ultimately useless views.

About the Author

Logan Anderson is a health professional, with a focus on working with individuals with special needs. He enjoys helping others become more independent on their wellness journey, to improve their health and quality of life. Logan has worked with individuals of varying abilities, shapes, and sizes, enjoying the idea of making fitness inclusive for everyone. Through working with numerous Special Olympics state programs, having conversations with a variety of seniors, and helping lower income, high risk individuals through fitness, he has gained invaluable insight in the importance in health for all. Fitness is all about working out at your own level and doing it for yourself. Working with seniors and individuals with varying disabilities has helped Logan realize this, and it has given him a unique perspective on the truly holistic nature that being healthy can bring to an individual.

Email: allstrongfitnessllc@gmail.com
Website: www.allstrongfitness.org

CHAPTER TWO
EARN IT

By Luis Araya
Professional Athlete, Water Polo
Athens, Greece | Stockton, California

There is always someone working harder than you.
—Mike Leabo

One of my life's biggest mottos is, "There will always be someone working harder than you." My first coach, the late Mike Leabo, said this to me. Let's back up to see where this motto took root in my life.

I was born and raised in Stockton, California. Growing up, I was always playing different sports and looking to win every competition. I began water polo when I was 10 years old because of a flier my mom found at her job. There was only one very small club in 2009 called B.A.G.S. Water Polo Club run by Coach Mike Leabo. That was the start of a journey that led me to play water polo in college. I attended University of the Pacific where the team remained in the top five for four years. This also included an NCAA National Championship appearance. As well as college, I competed globally, representing the USA, and I currently play water polo professionally in Europe.

One of the challenges I faced early on in my career was my lack of physical attributes, meaning I was not the biggest, strongest, or fastest kid. I was always playing against older kids, so developing and adapting to the bigger kids' style was more of a sink-or-swim experience, which could be pretty intimidating to an 11-year-old.

Mentally, I approached water polo differently from most other players due to the physical difference between older guys I was matched against and myself. In between tournament matches I watched other players to see what they liked to do and to notice their most common habits. I then went on to figure out why they made these mistakes. I loved this aspect of the sport because even when the game was over, I was still playing, knowing I would have to match up against them at some point. Building this hunger mentality was about knowing bigger and better competition was coming my way, and I wanted to be ready when the challenge came.

Growing up, I never hung out with friends or went to parties, especially in high school. Most days, I just tried to sneak into the pool, even when it was closed. I spent hours shooting by myself until I was too tired to continue. Within these times of being alone, I started to create a drive to just work, and I often thought of Coach Leabo's quote. I wanted to be that guy working harder than the others. My love for the game grew stronger during these times.

Another confrontation I faced throughout my career was becoming distracted by comparison. I found it hard not to compare my career achievements, support, connections, and more, with others. I focused on comparing myself in any area that I saw other players have an advantage. This is not an easy obstacle to overcome as many of us go through this phenomenon at some point in our careers. It can get frustrating comparing where we are with where we think we should be by looking at other's success.

To avoid falling into negative patterns from comparing myself with others, I worked intentionally on this and found that there are many methods to use to help me with this. In high school, I knew I would play against players who were ranked above me, so I simply made a list of the guys I knew I would see, and I'd go after each guy until, one by one, I crossed off everyone on the list as I became better than them. In this way, I didn't just compare myself and feel bad about not being as good as them in the moment. Rather, I worked hard to improve myself until I was better than them. This helped me prepare my mindset as I told myself, *Okay, everyone thinks he's better than me? We'll see how good he is when I play him.* This mindset moved me to always play harder and push myself past comfort.

Developing my skills helped build my confidence. I knew I couldn't be nervous about my lack of skills if I spent hours working on my craft. Sometimes, when people told me that I came across as cocky, I simply responded, "It's not cocky if you can back it up." My hard work built my confidence with small accomplishments such as pushing myself through a hard workout to defeating a top-tier team. This allowed me to stay focused on what I needed to do in order to be where I wanted to be in the future. I see it as each person has a box, and it's up to you to grow and develop your box to the best of your ability because no matter the resources or talent, no one will do it for you. That is why some distractions, such as parties or hanging out with friends all the time, can become the silent killers for athletes' success. The best athletes are the ones who spend extra time after training watching film, showing curiosity, working to continually improve, and self-isolating from others when needed. The goals that top athletes have are different from the goals of their friends, so decisions on priorities need to be made.

Another trial I faced throughout my career, specifically through my early 20s, was having moments of feeling lost. With these gray areas, some examples of things that were running through my mind were—*Am I on the correct path to play with the National Team? What should be my next move and where should I go after college? What is the best way to push myself to the next level? Am I where I should be in my career?*

These thoughts running in my head created a snowball effect such that I created stress and anxiety about things that were out of my control. The best way that I was taught to respond to this was to write down all the things I was concerned about and cross out all the things I couldn't control. This way I can focus on the things that are in my control.

Another strategy I use to strengthen my mind in order to practice patience is meditating for 10 to 30 minutes every morning. Talk about mindset; meditating became a magical tool for me. Meditating allows me to focus and prepare for the day. It's important to clear the mind and use the isolation as an opportunity to reinvest and build yourself up. The world is a tough place to live in, and every day you will run into some kind of obstacles. I've always believed that it is my responsibility to protect my dreams and goals and find the best way to tackle the day. For me, meditation is part of this, helping me as an athlete and as a person.

Olympic Development Program—Never Give Up

Through the years, USA Water Polo has hosted an annual event called the Olympic Development Program (ODP) championship. This tournament consists of kids with age groups ranging from 18 and under to 12 and under scattered throughout the USA. Each team is built according to the area participants live in, and the teams compete against other areas. At this tournament, USA scouts are placed at each pool to select the athletes they think best deserve to move on to the next round, which is called Selection Camp. The list of hundreds of athletes is reduced to 70 at Selection Camp. During this camp, athletes spend the weekend with Olympic and Junior National Team coaches going through drills, videos, and test sets. Usually at the end, there's a scrimmage to see which athletes stand out at the camp. Those athletes are selected to be on the Junior National Team representing the USA on the global stage.

My ODP debut started when I was 11, and I was competing with 14-year-olds. I can definitely say I was the smallest guy in the tournament, but I did what I could do and just tried my best. That was one of the first times in my career that I felt I got my butt kicked. After the tournament, the scouts made selections for athletes to move on to the next round. I was devastated when I wasn't chosen to move on, but I understood that I was only 11, and I was competing against kids older and bigger than me. At this early age, I faced my first obstacle of adversity, but I kept telling myself to try harder. Through the years, my methods to improve became more detail-oriented in terms of the skills I needed to develop to take things to the next level. I never gave up.

In my sixth year trying out, I made it to Selection Camp. On the last day of camp, they announced the final Junior Team roster, and they gave an evaluation of strengths, weaknesses, and improvements for each player. As the list of names was being read out loud, each athlete who was selected moved to the "final roster" side of the bleachers. Unfortunately, I was not selected even though I'd felt pretty confident about my performance over the three days. I decided to take the opportunity to speak with the head coach of the Junior Team at the time, Alex Rodriguez.

Coach Alex went through my evaluation and performance. I was told I was one spot away from making the roster. The reasons being that I was too small, not strong enough, not fast enough, and my defense was a weak point. Although a full year away, I made it my main priority to be a top prospect for the next ODP. I should add, I was filled with anger and frustration as well. Year after year, I'd seen the same players go ahead of me and have great opportunities to represent the USA. In hindsight, though, I can't thank Coach Alex enough for cutting me because I used what he told me as a big motivator throughout that year. I realized that hard work alone wouldn't be enough. I had to be smart about my work.

I decided to write down my weaknesses on sticky notes and put them everywhere. On my ceiling, bathroom mirror, closet mirror, fridge, and other places. I was so obsessed with this that it was the only thing on my mind for the entire year. I joined a swim team to get faster, lifting with a weight trainer, and staying in the pool longer, working on different skills.

In the following year, when the ODP coaches read off the list of athletes for the National Team, they made it all the way to the final round when I heard my name being called. I didn't react at first because this was my first time being selected and getting to move to the other side of the bleachers.

The takeaway from this experience is that I used the power of rejection to push me to be a better player, instead of giving up and making excuses. Throughout the years, I hadn't been the only player that was rejected. I saw new faces each year come and go. I was sure that If I stuck it out, eventually I would get my opportunity. A big part of who I am today came from this moment alone. I learned from rejection, decided to mentally and physically attack my athletic shortcomings, and I became better.

The 666 Program

In my offseason, I went through a heavy training cycle in which my body took a heavy toll, but the most important aspect was pushing my mind to its limitations. I have what is called a 666 program. This means that for six months I would train for six days a week for six hours a day. I started every morning at 4 a.m., usually in the gym lifting for two hours. Afterwards, I would come home and eat, recover, and have a swim set for an hour. I'd swim three to five kilometers a day. I would eat, recover, and relax only to go back to the pool to train for another three hours.

With this vigorous training, it is not only a matter of physically pushing yourself but mentally becoming stronger and sharper. Self-discipline allows this. It's easy to say, "I don't need to go to the gym at 4 a.m.," or "I don't need to jump in the pool at 11 p.m. for three hours." Having discipline completely cuts out all the bad habits of taking shortcuts, whether it be a day off, a workout, a set, or a rep. I never negotiated with myself because I made a deal to hold myself accountable to the highest standard.

In between my trainings, I would read autobiographies of athletes and their journeys and how they overcame their defiant moments. Every person's career is different, and it's important to learn from others because you never know when you might run into a similar issue at some point. Elite athletes have learned and treated their career as a sponge, absorbing as much as they can from the best.

It's important to surround yourself with a support cast of people who help push you to be the best version of yourself. I have been fortunate to have a great support cast of family helping me achieve dreams and goals in my career. There are many coaches in my career who have helped me learn different aspects to the sport of water polo. Just to list a few, my first coach, Mike Leabo, helped me fall in love with water polo and created a foundation for me. Dragan Bakic, another coach I had early on in my career, pushed me to be more disciplined, and he always put me with the older age groups to challenge me. Jeff Hoernart, head coach of Saint Mary's water polo, helped build a creativity to my style of play and provided me with massive support, so I could improve. Nikos Venetopoulos, former Olympiacos water polo player and coach, believed in my abilities and gave me the opportunities to learn from his experience. We watched film together and analyzed opponents. Mrs. Gillespie, my English teacher at Saint Mary's high school, had a quote that stuck with me, stating, "Greatness lies with those who make the best of what they have."

Somewhere along the journey in everyone's career, there will be mentors, coaches, teammates, and teachers. But it's up to you on what you can learn from each one that will help you take that one step closer to achieving your goals.

At many points in our careers, our dreams may start to fade away. As challenges and adversity become bigger, it's easier to stick with something easier where the salary is stable, comfortable, and reliable. In order to become a peak performance athlete, there needs to be risk, chaos, and uncertainty. With the good, we must take the difficult. Risk, chaos, and uncertainty helps us adapt and deal with bigger issues to make us better in the long run.

Ultimately, my goal is to go to the Olympics and represent my country. In this route, there are a lot of mental roadblocks to tackle, but along the way, I have learned many lessons and methods to help me face adversity. Without a doubt, the most important lesson to learn as a young athlete is to become a sponge and absorb as much knowledge as you can from those whom you aspire to be like. Let their example bring out the best in you. It's important to always be curious and ask questions about things that interest you. Everyone is going through their own obstacles on the road toward success. It's critical to keep an open mind and try out new things. I was never a fan of meditation until I actually did it; now it's part of my daily routine. I grew up in a non-water-polo family, as a first generation college graduate, and with no previous connections within the sport, but here I am, playing as a professional.

With the right mindset, anything is possible. It is truly about making the best with what you've got. I challenge you to keep working and persevering toward your goals, as I will do the same. The best is yet to come.

About the Author

Luis Araya's roots began in the hardy streets of Stockton, California, where he grew up a tenacious and determined athlete. Water polo has been his life ever since he began at the age of 10. Luis attended Saint Mary's High School and University of the Pacific where he majored in business marketing. Throughout his career, Luis has represented the USA in both Junior and Senior National Team events across the globe. Currently, Luis is playing water polo professionally overseas and looks to inspire those who wish to chase their dreams and goals while tackling the hardships of adversity. Luis would like to dedicate this chapter to his mom.

LinkedIn: https://www.linkedin.com/in/luis-araya-c/

CHAPTER THREE

A CHAMPION'S MINDSET WHEN BREAKING THROUGH ADVERSITY

By David Arsenault
Founder, Champions for Life, Taekwondo Champion
Baie-d'Urfé, Quebec, Canada

We all admire the incredible feats that top performers achieve in sport, business, or other aspects of life. What is it about these "champions" that makes them stand out and have such success in the face of great challenges and adversity? As you might guess, there are many factors that contribute to success, like passion and determination, work ethic and perseverance, previous experience and goal setting, and having the right people around you.

Perseverance is the act of pushing through adversity until we achieve a goal. Along the meandering path and pursuit to our objectives, perseverance is what keeps us on the road to our goals. During critical times of the journey, we may all face major obstacles and seemingly insurmountable odds that were not factored into our thoughts and plans. How do we overcome these physical, mental, and or emotional roadblocks?

In this chapter I share my experience at the 2000 Canadian National Taekwondo Championships where I overcame a challenge that I did not anticipate, much like we all have to do when we are faced with adversity in our lives.

It had been 10 years of competing at the national level when I finally won the 2000 Canadian Taekwondo Championships in the lightweight division, often the largest category amongst the eight weight divisions. Being 29 years old and having put countless hours in preparation and dedication to a life as a martial artist and as an athlete, I decided that it would be my last nationals regardless of the outcome. Until that moment, I had no regrets and was willing to walk from competition, knowing that I had given it my all.

A year earlier, I had a disappointing loss at the 1999 national championship when I'd been favored to win. With my head hanging low, one of my fellow teammates came to me to say that he was taking a year off from competing in order to put together a small group of athletes who would make a run for the 2000 national championships. Until then, I had been a nomad, training as much and as often as possible at various clubs and with my closest friend. I decided to join.

I trusted in my coach and bonded with my new training partners, as we wasted no time getting to work. My perseverance, dedication, and sacrifice brought me once again to the starting line at the 2000 nationals. How do you do something you have never done before? As those who have been at the top of the podium know, it's not a sure thing and if you don't try, you won't get there. The only way forward is to put one foot in front of the other, keeping the butterflies and nerves in check. So, it began for me at the competition by starting off with a relatively easy win.

The second match was going well until the second round when I cut my foot right to the bone on the outside of my ankle. Adrenaline has a good way to numb pain for a short period to help you get through pretty much anything. The same was true for my opponent who lost his two front teeth in the exchange. I won the fight in the end.

After the match, I was brought to the competition's medical booth where there was a doctor and two interns who wasted no time getting to work. Until then, I had no idea what medical staples were. By the time they were done, there were six staples on an inch-and-a-half gash on my ankle. It then dawned on me that I needed to go on to fight in the semi-finals. The doctors said that they'd thought I was done for the day and hadn't known I was still in the competition. They said that they were sorry, but there was no way that I would be able to continue to compete that day. They said, "We cannot let you compete with your ankle in that condition."

There was no question in my mind that I was done. It took the next 20 minutes to convince them that I was fit to continue. I assured them that I would not be kicking with that part of my foot—not true—and that they could pad me up in a way that would protect the cut and staples. I ended up writing a letter, taking all responsibility and waiving them of any liability for my actions. The main doctor finally signed the letter and led the tape job on my foot, and I was good to go.

I don't know how long it was before my next match, but it was certainly long enough for the swelling and pain to settle in. It was also enough time to let doubt creep in. Championship rounds are tough enough without injuries. Being my last nationals and my first time with an injury of this magnitude, I had my work cut out for me.

I was called on deck to fight against an up-and-coming star from my province whom I had not faced before. He was hungry, had studied me well, and knew I was hurt. This was the moment that things could go either way for me, but I was resolved to do my best. To be honest, knowing that true virtue is doing your best regardless of the outcome, it's easy to rest on that moral. There is a fine line between performing at your peak and winning or losing in competition. I remember a moment when I was honestly ready to throw in the towel with my injury, which would have been a good excuse to bow out at that stage.

The most critical moment of the competition, and my athletic career for that matter, was when I stepped onto the mat for the semi-final. I wanted to give my best effort under the current circumstances, but most of all, I did not want to make excuses in the end. Facing their fears is the true nature of a warrior and expression of their indomitable spirit, an unconquerable attitude that is impossible to vanquish.

At the end of the second round, I was down by four points, which was a significant gap to make up in the last round in Taekwondo at that time. During the break before the final round, my coach could sense that there was no question of my giving up or giving in. We exchanged a few words, and he said, "Keep doing what you're doing, you got this." I ended up winning the match by scoring clearly and not letting my opponent score another point. To his credit, he went on to be national champion in subsequent years.

Besides the injury, the game plan that my coach and I crafted was going precisely as planned. It was a true collective effort that resulted in impeccable conditioning with a strategy and tactics that were on point. One of my team-mates had realized her dream and won the title in her division the day before.

A few hours later, at center stage during the finals, I was faced again with the fear and doubt of performing through pain against an equally dedicated and worthy athlete who deserved his shot at the title every bit as much as I did. It was the first time we had met each other in competition, and we both wanted it as much as the other. The winner and 2000 national champion would represent Canada at the Pan American Taekwondo Championships in Aruba and the World Cup in Vietnam.

When I got called to present myself for the finals, a senior master came to see me and my coach to say that he would coach me in the finals. Like many sports, Taekwondo is not immune from politics and egos. It didn't take any time for my coach to look at me and say, "It doesn't matter who will be coaching you in the final. You have everything it takes." So it was, the master coached me.

I hardly remember the match aside from the fact that we both fought hard. You may be picturing me hobbling on one foot like the Karate Kid and doing a spectacular swan kick finish. There was no such moment. Both my feet were firmly on the ground, and I hit my opponent with my injured foot as hard and as often as I could. In the end, the match finished in a tie. It was up to the center referee to decide who was most aggressive and had superior technique. This person would be declared winner.

Win or lose, the real victory for me in the end was to face my greatest challenge, *myself*, summarized by my fear of the outcome. It would have been easy to give in to the doubt and fear of not winning after nine years of competing at that level. It would have been perfectly acceptable to say that I was too injured to continue. I could have been thrown off the gameplan by not having my coach behind me in the final match. We create our own challenges, and, in the end, it is ourselves that we must overcome if we want to perform at peak levels. It's not about winning a medal or a title. It's not about facing a strong opponent. Indomitable spirit is about doing your best when there is no guarantee that you will succeed.

There is no virtue in being fearless in the eyes of others. What is virtuous is making no excuses to do your absolute best, regardless of the outcome. I often hear people say that you must give 110 percent. To me, there is no greater effort than your best. Indomitable spirit is making no excuses to be all you can be in the face of great adversity. We all have the capacity to do this in any aspect of our lives.

In the 200 Championships, I won the competition and finally had the honour to represent Canada on the national team. That year, I finished my athletic career with what was to be three more international competitions. I also got married to my life partner and started my career as a strength and conditioning coach to world champion and professional athletes. The opponent whom I fought in the final won nationals the following year. He was a true warrior in his own right. Like me, he never gave up even though it also took him 10 years to reach the pinnacle of his career.

About the Author

David Arsenault is the founder and executive director of the Champions for Life Foundation. This is a charity, passionate about helping children live healthy, active lifestyles and assisting communities in need. You can find out more about the Champions for Life Foundation in the section below.

With over 30 years of experience in the field of physical activity and athletics, David is also a former international athlete in Taekwondo, a professional trainer, and a visionary change-maker. David is dedicated to providing a "transformation" in the lives of those he helps.

David is a happy husband and proud father who has devoted his life's work to teaching children how to move to the best of their abilities. His personal journey is guided by his love for movement and sharing his passion with others.

Email: d.arsenault@championsforlife.ca
Website: https://www.championsforlife.ca

CHAPTER FOUR
LOVE THE PROCESS

By Norma Bastidas
Guinness World Record Holder, Longest Triathlon
Los Angeles, California

Winners embrace hard work. They love the discipline of it, the trade-off they're making to win. Losers, on the other hand, see it as punishment. And that's the difference.
—Lou Holtz

Sometimes it is hard to pinpoint the exact moment when you stop reacting to the circumstances in your life and instead start acting in a conscious manner to actively influence certain outcomes. As for me, I have a vivid recollection of that exact moment. Growing up, I had a difficult childhood and even more difficult youth. While I developed certain skills early in life that would help me become a record-breaking athlete much later (like the belief I could overcome anything), I was still missing the next mindset tool that would take me from passively reacting to challenges to taking charge of the direction of my life.

Being tough enough to take as many punches as life can give you is not the same as being a skilled fighter who wins the fight. For me, the skill of developing the mindset of a champion came a lot later in life. The mindset that helped my transformation from victim to champion came at a moment in my life when I decided that living for survival was no longer something I wanted to rely on. Instead, I realized I wanted so much more. This moment for me was when my oldest son was diagnosed with an incurable visual condition called cone-rod dystrophy, and he started to lose his sight at a rapid rate. This was the moment when the price became too high for me to just shy away and fall back into what I considered a normal life.

I was a single mother of two sons, aged 11 and nine, living in a foreign country without any family to lean on for support. What soon followed were months of confusion, pain, loss of income as a result of being fired from my job, and then finally full-blown depression. I have suffered depression since age 12, a co-occurrence of developing post-traumatic stress disorder from surviving years of abuse. At age 38, I was used to being in that state of helplessness, but this time I made a choice that I had not taken before. For the first time, I was not going to lie down and take the beating; I was not going to feel victimized by my circumstances. I was, instead, going to stand up and start fighting for the life I knew I deserved because this time, I was not only fighting for myself, but also for my sons. I decided I not only wanted to survive the challenge, but I wanted to thrive in spite of it. So early one morning, when the familiar feeling of insomnia came knocking, I decided to lace up my running shoes and go on a run.

Before my son's diagnosis, I was a fit mom who looked to stay relatively active since my dad had died of a heart attack at a young age. However, running was something I didn't do very often, nor was it something I ever saw myself doing at a high level. During this time back in 2006, my role in athletics was relegated to step aerobics, a bit of tennis, and any other type of sports a suburban mom was encouraged to pursue to lose weight. Then, that one snowy morning around 5 a.m., I went for a run, mostly so my kids wouldn't hear me cry. That morning I set out to find a place where I could be sad, but unexpectedly I found a place that made me smile.

For many weeks, it was the same. I would wake up, feel sadness and fear creeping in, lace up, go out on a run, cry for a while, then get a boost of optimism, and return home with a refreshed and positive outlook to my current situation. As I developed this routine, the weeks turned to months, and the time spent crying got shorter while the time spent running got longer and longer. Within a few months, I decided I was ready to run my first half-marathon. I finished it with a time of one hour and 39 minutes.

As I continued my routine of daily runs, my best friend had recently returned from running the Boston Marathon, and she began encouraging me to try and qualify for the next year's race by doing well in the upcoming local full marathon. She told me that if I was able to qualify, she would pay my way to the race, and we could run it together as a celebration of my 40th birthday. So about eight months after I started my running journey, I ran my first full marathon and, to my surprise, qualified for Boston. This was my first big experience with running, and it was one I would not soon forget.

Immediately when I returned, I decided to run another race before the summer was over. Given my limited resources, both in time and money, it had to be close to where I was living. My search resulted in only very few races, but amongst the handful of 5Ks and 10Ks, there was one race that stood out, the Canadian Death Race, a 125-kilometer (78-mile) race in a remote town called Grand Cache in Alberta. I don't know what possessed me to call and see if I could actually get a spot. I suspect I still had a fear that I might go back to feeling the terrible sadness that had been my constant companion the year prior. However, I did choose to call and subsequently received a spot as a soloist in the race. Only three weeks after my first marathon, I was set to run my first ultramarathon.

My attempt at the race was as good as I could have expected for my first try. I couldn't possibly wrap my mind around finishing such a distance, but I wanted to give it my best shot and see what I was capable of. Back then, ultramarathon running was still rare, and I had never actually met anybody who had done such a race, so when I didn't finish the race, I wasn't disappointed or surprised. What did surprise me was that I managed to run 59 miles before falling in a creek in the middle of the night and having to DNF (race code for Did Not Finish) because I was showing signs of hypothermia. Despite this unexpected end, my mind never gave up! When they were bringing me down the mountain, I was thinking, "This is it. This is what I want to do the rest of my life." Never in my life had I felt so alive.

That night was the birth of my new life as an ultrarunner, and eventually an endurance athlete. The most amazing transformation was that as one part of my life improved because I now had something that was giving me immense joy, it started to spill over in every part of my life. I no longer viewed challenges as problems but rather as opportunities of undiscovered potential.

Over the last 14 years, I have run ultramarathons across all continents, setting the record for the fastest known time for my effort. I have climbed some of the highest peaks around the world, and most notably, I broke the Guinness World Record for the Longest Triathlon in 2014.

The reason I like to diversify myself and switch sports is because I am most interested in mastering my mind and its ability, and for me, a great way to do that is by starting again from the bottom and applying what I have learned in different sports, tweaking the lessons along the way. When I feel my mind isn't growing as much as my body, I find value in undertaking a different challenge that forces me to have that same mindset as when I first began running.

There are many factors that play into the success of our ambitions. Some are beyond our control, so they shouldn't be considered, but sadly that is exactly where a lot of athletes spend most of their energy, worrying about the "what ifs" of every new challenge. If I could give one piece of advice to anyone looking to develop the mindset of a champion, it's this—*learn to love the grind, not just tolerate it, or even understand it, but genuinely love the grind.* Do not view training as a means to an end, but rather as an integral part of your journey.

The reason why I was able to qualify for the Boston Marathon on my first try was because I had spent so much of my time running and embracing the grind. By the time I considered running my first race, I was running so much that I was averaging 100 miles per week and loving every moment of it. I fell in love with the sport and did it for the love of it. The races were just a bonus for me at that point. For my first ultramarathon race, what some might see as a disappointing end, instead, left me exhilarated and excited to train for next year's race because it meant another year of doing what I loved to do. The following year at the Canadian Death Race, not only did I finish, I placed as the ninth female overall and won for my age group.

My best performances as an athlete have always been after a period of consistent, high-quality training, where I can not only work on my abilities, but my mind as well. I still love getting lost in the thick of the training. I long for the countless hours spent honing a skill and perfecting my game, something that is now strange in the age of instant gratification, fueled by social media where we are only exposed to the outcome and not the journey.

True greatness takes time; it's the sum of thousands of small efforts done consistently that amounts to an unshakeable mind. Once, a long time ago, at an event, I met the late Walter Gretzky, father of Wayne Gretzky, arguably the best hockey player of all time. I asked him if it was true that he built a hockey rink in his backyard for his son when he was little. Walter told me that it was true, but that it was not because he wanted his son to be the best hockey player in the world, he built the ring because his son loved hockey so much that he would beg to stay after practice, so he could play some more. He and his wife found sitting in a cold ice rink for hours miserable, so he built the rink in his backyard, so his son could do what he loved whenever he wanted. Wayne Gretzky loved playing hockey; he would practice not just until he got it right, but instead, he would practice over and over until he wouldn't get it wrong. You see—if you fall in love with the process, you too will become unstoppable.

About the Author

In 2014, Norma Bastidas, a single mother and a survivor of sexual violence and human trafficking, broke the Guinness World Record for Longest Triathlon after swimming, biking, and running 3,762 miles (6,054 km) from Cancún, Mexico, to Washington, D.C., USA. She is an ultra-adventurer who views this incredible athletic feat as a metaphor for the incredible trials faced every day by the survivors of human trafficking and sexual violence. Norma's mission is to educate and empower, demonstrating to the world that one's past does not dictate one's future. She hopes to prove that everyday people are capable of making extraordinary strides in the fight against the problems facing the world today.

Twitter and Instagram: @ultrarunwild

CHAPTER FIVE
WHITE BELT MENTALITY

By Emily Buckley
Dual Sport Collegiate Athlete, CrossFit Competitor
Brooklyn, New York

Be brave enough to suck at something new.
—Unknown

I was in Florida, which was a nice break from the freezing weather in New England. As a team, we had been practicing in hail, snow, and freezing temperatures for a few weeks. Before the official season started, we had two pre-season games in the Sunshine State against a couple of nationally ranked teams. I was standing on the sideline with the ball in my stick. I was nervous. As I stood there scanning the field, looking for an open teammate, I saw all of them running in the opposite direction. I was confused by this. Surely someone was going to check towards me, so I could inbound the ball. Panic and uncertainty set in. Turns out lacrosse is one of the few sports that inbounding the ball is not necessary. Instead, you can run straight onto the field once the official blows the whistle. What an embarrassing moment. I was standing there, at my first collegiate lacrosse game with my flawed understanding of the sport on display for everyone to see.

I grew up playing soccer as my only sport. I spent my entire childhood obsessing over soccer. I would dribble the ball up and down the streets of New York City, where I grew up. I would go to multiple practices a day, practice on my own, and do crunches in bed after my parents told me to go to sleep.

I was obsessed and dedicated. My goal was to play soccer in college, and I accomplished that goal. I was a starting player and a leading goal scorer, what a dream come true!

One day after our soccer season finished for the year, I received an email from the lacrosse coach at my college. It's an email that I later printed out and hung in my dorm room through undergraduate and graduate school. It is an email that I still have to this day. I keep it in a box with all of my prized athletic possessions over the years. There are two meaningful sentences in that email that have been highlighted with a yellow marker for the last 12 years:

- "I obviously think highly of you as an athlete. And I feel confident that you could help us be a better team. Your work rate, your dedication to your sport and your ability to lead by example are all things that I know our team could benefit from."
- "Things happen for a reason, and when all is said and done, you need to make decisions that make you happy. Or in this case might make you happy."

The thought of playing a new sport was intimidating to me. I had established myself as a soccer player, and our team's leading goal scorer. I loved that sense of accomplishment and that identity for myself. I was nervous to even entertain the idea of starting something where I wouldn't be one of the best players. After a bit of thought, I ended up saying yes.

I knew nothing about the game of lacrosse. When I showed up to my first practice, I felt insecure because I had no idea what I was doing. I was sure after that first practice, I was going to quit. I was so used to being one of the best soccer players on our team that when I was undoubtedly the worst player at lacrosse practice, I felt self-conscious. As I walked off the field, I thought there was no way that I'd want to put myself through that feeling day after day. Afterwards, I went back to my dorm room, showered, and thought about it a bit more. I decided I would go back the next day. That decision making process went on every day for the first two weeks. I kept showing up. That was the best decision my 19-year-old self could have made.

The second-best decision was made shortly after. I decided to have, what I call now, a white belt mentality. I decided I would learn and practice as much as I could, so that I was prepared for the season. I attached myself to my teammates. I watched them in practice, how they moved their sticks, what they did when they didn't have the ball, how they communicated. I hung out with them to better understand terminology and the way they thought about the game. I listened to their feedback while we watched film of games from years past. I did as much as I could to learn and improve in the short few months we had before the season actually started.

I owe a lot to those teammates who welcomed me onto the team. I can only imagine how frustrating it could have been to have someone who had never played before join your nationally ranked college team. To say that I stepped onto a team that was way out of my league would be a vast understatement. We had multiple players who had been named to All-American teams. In all fairness, I never became a truly great lacrosse player. However, I did earn a starting spot on the roster and was able to contribute to the team's success for the next three years. At one point, our team's defense was ranked fourth in the country, and I played a defensive position every minute of that season.

So, how did I go from knowing absolutely nothing to being a contributing member of the team? The answer is my mindset. I had a white belt mentality.

White belt mentality originates from the traditional martial arts belt system. Every beginner starts off as a white belt. The white belt represents a lack of knowledge. As you learn more, you advance in belt color. When you're a white belt, you are expected to be a student of the art. You show up every day, looking to learn something from every experience you have. You show up with humility, vulnerability, and an eagerness to learn. I love taking the idealism of the white belt innocence and applying it to the world outside of martial arts.

White Belt Mentality Pillars

There are three main pillars to white belt mentality:

1. **Be vulnerable**. Be open to learn from those who know more than you, and respect what you don't know.
2. **Become a student of your craft**. Devote yourself to deliberate practice and intensive detail.
3. **Focus on what is in your control**. Work on maximizing your potential in the things you can control.

White belt mentality is having the vulnerability to become a true learner of your subject matter. It is devoting yourself to what other people would see as meaningless details. It's focusing on what is inside of your control while maximizing your potential.

I was deeply, deeply interested in learning absolutely everything I could about lacrosse. I took learning about it to an absurd level. I carried my stick with me everywhere. I would bring it around campus; I would bring it to class; it wouldn't leave my side. There are pictures of me napping in the dorm room with my lacrosse stick placed next to me.

Adopting the white belt mentality meant I would allow myself to be a sponge in this new world and be vulnerable enough in front of my teammates to ask them for help. I was so focused at practice that if anyone said anything unrelated to lacrosse, I would ask them to wait until after practice because I was afraid I'd miss something Coach was saying.

I dedicated hours after practice to throwing the ball against the wall of our athletic center to work on my throwing and catching skills. I did this every day. One night after practice, as I was throwing the ball against the wall, our athletic director came outside and told me that they could hear the thud of the ball inside of the office for the last hour and that it was time to go back to the dorms. I just found another wall.

I even went as far as learning how to string lacrosse sticks. This isn't a necessary skill and certainly didn't help my physical ability to play at all, but I thought that if I familiarized myself with how the stick was strung, my knowledge there would somehow become better. I would go for extra runs outside of practice to improve my conditioning, and I would run with my stick in my hands.

Adopting this mindset has allowed me to excel in many ways and has instilled in me the confidence that I can do anything if I approach it with the pillars listed above. It can be implemented in anything and everything. I've found great success in utilizing this mentality to achieve peak physical performance, from competing at the CrossFit Games to competing for USA Weightlifting to finding a new passion in rock climbing.

White belt mentality was very important for me during my rock-climbing journey. It led me to hitting milestone achievements in an extremely short time period. There is a highly respected climbing grade (difficulty rating of a climb), which is labeled 5.12 on the Yosemite Decimal System. It is a grade that people train for years to achieve, and many never do. In less than eight months, I went from being a novice to successfully climbing my first 5.12 climb! I attribute this to approaching the steep learning curve with a white belt mentality. This is the mental tool I use to perform at peak levels more quickly than most would consider possible.

When I first started climbing, I dove head first into learning as much as I could. I had a friend who was a great climber, and, once a week, we would climb together. She would help me pinpoint areas that I needed to work on, and I would then spend the rest of the week, night and day, working on those weaknesses. I would find myself at home sitting on the floor practicing clipping quickdraws and tying knots late into the evening.

One of the great things about white belt mentality is that the act of becoming a student of your craft increases your respect for the sport. Rock climbing can be very dangerous, and it deserves the utmost respect. Having a deep respect for a dangerous sport can help you gauge what limits are safe to push and alert you when you need to back down. There is a mental aspect of climbing in which something can feel scary, but it actually is relatively safe. And there are other times when something can feel safe and is actually not. Knowing the situation you're in and having a sound understanding of your ability is key to your survival. White belt mentality allows your ego to get out of the way, so you can assess your abilities clearly.

Within a year and a half of learning how to climb, I did my first free solo ascent of one of the flatirons in Boulder, Colorado. I was ecstatic and elated when I got to the top of the over 600-foot exposed climb. I felt accomplished and excited to do more. I followed it up by doing six other free solo ascents. Free soloing, which is climbing without the protection of a rope, pushes your mental capacity. It forces you to focus, be humble, and respect the mountains. Since focus, vulnerability, and respect are pillars of white belt mentality, I felt I was well equipped mentally and physically to take on this challenge.

When you fully embrace white belt mentality, it unlocks doors that you couldn't otherwise imagine. This is not limited to only the world of sports performance. It can unlock doors in the business world as well. This is a mentality that I've taken and used in professional settings. It has allowed me to become confident in my approach to starting new positions, branching out into new industries, and learning from others. At 30, I became the chief operating officer of a multi-million-dollar company headquartered in New York City.

I think back to the scared, embarrassed, and nervous college athlete that I was, standing on the sideline, realizing I didn't know the rules of the sport I was playing. While that moment was uncomfortable, I'm thankful for that experience and the mindset that I've gained from it.

I would encourage anyone interested in growing any aspect of their life to adapt the white belt mentality. Excellence can only be achieved by having the humility and vulnerability to know that you need to learn and use focus and devotion to make it happen. With focus, dedication, and a learner's mindset, peak performance can be quickly achieved in any activity you pursue.

About the Author

Emily Buckley is an operations executive, a CrossFit Games Athlete, and an outdoor enthusiast. She was born and raised in Brooklyn, New York, and has dedicated her life to sports, fitness, and maximizing her potential. Throughout her life, she's focused on a broad spectrum of fitness modalities: kickboxing, Tae Kwon Do, Olympic weightlifting, CrossFit, rock climbing, mountain biking, and mountain running. She's interested in all types of physical challenges, and as a true believer in having a growth mindset, she tries to learn new sports as often as possible.

Email: emilybuckley2@gmail.com

CHAPTER SIX

SOCIOLOGY AND PEAK PERFORMANCE

By Tarek Charaf, PhD
Peak Performance Coach, Sports Development Adviser
Doha, Qatar

Sociology plays a direct role in the development of thought and behavior. It has a general impact over the masses and personal impact over individuals. Humans are born with a *tabula rasa* cognitive mind, just like a new empty hard drive ready to be filled with data, any data it is presented with. Even before birth, an embryo starts registering data through the environment of their mother's womb. As the child is exposed to life outside the womb, they develop a cognitive process of thought, directly associated with the immediate surrounding society and environment.

The first influencers are the parents (or persons taking this function). Children are directly affected by their parents, whom they blindly trust and look to for guidance (coaching) for their achievements in life. This parent-child relation, where the parent is the individual giving mentorship and, therefore, imposing approval or disapproval guidelines over the child, becomes the child's main source of validation.

Children develop a dependency on validation and approval from their parents, especially when they are in a process of developing self-confidence. They need the approval of their parental guides, coaches, teachers, and mentors to affirm them as conforming to the "proper" norms. Unfortunately, those norms are not restricted to the parents only. An entire society imposes its norms on the individual. In this way, there's a kind of enforced conformation of the individual to the "system" in place by that specific society.

For example, a child born into an extremely conservative society will most probably develop a similar conservative way of thinking, as that child is constantly bombarded with such extreme cues from their validation sources. In this way, the child receives positive validation from others for conservative cognition and behavior.

The same thing would apply to a child born into a liberal society. The child would then most likely develop a liberal cognitive and behavioral process, due to the positive validation for liberal cognition and behavior. For example, consider a child born and raised in conservative Kandahar, Afghanistan, in comparison to a child born and raised in liberal Stockholm, Sweden.

Therefore, society has great impact and largely affects the shaping of the cognitive and behavioral processes in a person. Adding to it is some people's constant need for validation. When a person actually does not work to develop an independent and clear mindset (intrinsic motivation), the external factors (extrinsic motivation) become their main focus. Those factors directly impact and control their mood, thoughts, and behavior. In a way, the person becomes trapped by their need for constant appraisal from others in order to validate themselves as successful, appreciated, loved, respected, and so on.

Sociology and Sport—The Triangle and Circles

In sport, such as in life, an athlete or any other person can be defined as a performance triangle. This triangle is composed of the following three aspects, as seen below: talent, physical readiness, and mental readiness.

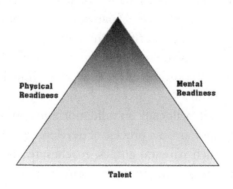

Each and every living being (not humans only) has a certain leading edge and benefit of some sort. This advantage is called talent. Plants, for example, have the "talent" to recycle oxygen, clean the air, cure ailments, or simply beautify the scenery. Humans, in parallel, have a multitude of talents, be it educational, vocational, professional, artistic or other. Even theft can be classified as a talent if the person involved is a very good thief. Talents, as such, can be perceived either as positive or negative, but remain talents nevertheless.

A person can have a multitude of talents at the same time, and can focus on more than one talent simultaneously. The same person can, therefore, have talent at many levels. Michael Jordan, considered the best basketball athlete of his time, was also a professional golfer and baseball player, who switched between sports during his career. Nasser Saleh Al Attyiah, from Qatar, is a world rally champion who also won a bronze medal in shooting at the London Olympic Games in 2012. Also, he is a confirmed horseman and motorcycle pilot. What these people have in common, which differentiates them from the masses, is their ability to optimize their triangle, focusing on reaching their peak talent performance, peak physical readiness, and peak mental readiness.

Reaching the peak and staying there is, unfortunately, not an easy task. It can take several years, if not a lifetime, for a person to excel in one single talent. As life is clearly imperfect, perfection is almost impossible to reach (constant 100 percent); yet excellence is a beautiful second option (constant 70 percent to 80 percent, leaving a small acceptable percentage of human error). With focusing on optimizing their triangle, a person can ensure they get the closest possible to perfection while understanding that excelling and giving their best, as opposed to perfection, is the actual final objective.

Since humans live in society and are in direct daily contact with the outside world, it is only normal for them to be influenced by society in one way or another. Athletes, for example, are directly and indirectly affected by a multitude of factors that surround their sports careers and personal lives. They are under the direct influence of their family and friends, coaching team, sports club, school, or athletic career.

These athletes are also affected by many indirect factors such as weather, availability of proper training and competition venues, the existence of governmental support programs, the possibility of securing funding or sponsorship to cover the costs of training and competing, whether the country in which they live provides a modern sports medicine program and follow-up for athletes, and so on.

A person's triangle is clearly influenced by many external factors that can affect it either positively or negatively. Those factors directly influence the athlete, and also the athlete can influence some of those factors. The closer the external factor is to the athlete, the bigger and closer is the mutual sphere of influence. The farther the external factor is to the athlete, the smaller and farther is the mutual sphere of influence. For example, an athlete is directly affected by their coach and has, in return, a direct influence over their coach through daily or weekly interaction. An example of a smaller and more distant sphere of influence would be that an athlete has little or no control over the weather or sports legislation in their country.

What peak performance teaches is the exact nature of the relationship between the most important external factors to the athlete and the level of control the athlete has over those factors. Based on prioritization and level of control, in addition to overcoming dichotomous thinking, achieving peak performance requires the individual to understand and optimize their control over external factors.

The figure below overlays the triangle and some of the most relevant external factors that affect an athlete's career:

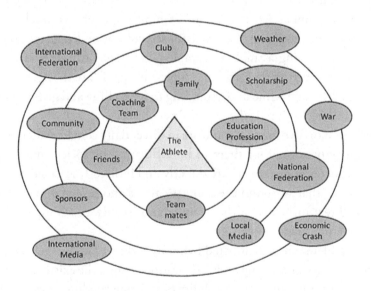

In the graphic above, the position of the external factors vis-à-vis the athlete is based on their priority and direct sphere of influence towards the athlete and vice versa. The closer the circle in which an external factor is positioned, the stronger the direct influence of that external factor is on the athlete. For example, an athlete has, by far, more influence and impact on their close circle of family and friends, rather than the global economy or the start of a war. Even still, it is interesting how athletes (and so many of us) often repeatedly focus on what they cannot control rather than what they can control.

This tendency can be very destructive in the long run, as focusing on what they cannot control often results in developing negative emotions such as frustration, disappointment, anger, and anxiety. When it happens regularly over time, it can lead to the development of a chronic negative process of thought, behavior, and emotions.

Because of this, it is of the utmost importance for athletes to learn and understand what they can and cannot control, so as to optimize their resilience and minimize their frustration.

Religion and Philosophy in Sociology

Religion, whether we want it to or not, plays a direct role in the cognitive and behavioral processes of individuals and the masses. According to the Hartford Institute, sociology of religion is the study of the beliefs, practices, and organizational forms of religion. Sociologists of religion study every aspect of religion, from what is believed, to how people act while in worship and while living out their stated convictions.

Historically the study of religion was central to the discipline of sociology with early influential scholars, such as Emile Durkheim and Max Weber, writing extensively on the role and function of religion in human society. Social scientists who study religion today perform a vital function in helping the general public make sense of the rise of religious themes and influences in television, political conflicts, and public and personal issues. The discipline of the sociology of religion has much to teach about how religion functions for the individual and in society. As for philosophy and sociology, they complement each other, giving a deeper understanding of human behavior, social norms, morality, and the workings of the mind.

Peak performance uses philosophy, religion, and sociology in order to explain to the individual the notions of perfection and excellence. This, in return, assists the individual to set achievable goals and understand that perfection doesn't exist.

Peak performance simplifies the notion of religion by setting two main categories, believers and non-believers. For believers, in what relates to the single-God religions, the story of Adam and Eve is used to explain the notion of perfection. As this story is discussed and agreed upon by Judaism, Christianity, and Islam, peak performance reminds us that Adam and Eve were living in paradise, also known as the "perfect" place. After eating the apple, they are both cast out of paradise—the land of perfection—and onto earth to be tried for their lack of loyalty and disobedience to God. As the earthly life is described with successes and failures, it is clear that life on earth is, therefore, not perfect.

As such, the first mistake we, humans, make is to expect perfection on earth. We innately know through religion that perfection does not exist in this life. However, through optimizing the triangle and the influence of the circles, we can achieve excellence, which is the closest possible to perfection. The main difference between perfection and excellence is the fact that perfection does not allow for mistakes, whereas excellence allows us to use mistakes to learn and progress, with the ultimate objective of transcendence, meaning being at our best.

As for multiple-God religions, they all clearly note the imperfection of life on this earth. Therefore, they make it much easier to explain the notion of imperfection and the aspiration to excellence.

For non-believers, it makes it even easier for peak performance to explain the nonexistence of imperfection on earth. My personal example used with athletes and clients is the simple example that had life been perfect, we would all have excellent health, six packs, and five billion American dollars in the bank, which is not the case. For more skeptical people, a simple reminder of all the misfortunes, famine, poverty, disease, and injustice since the birth of humankind is enough to connect their cognition process to reality and make them realize that perfection does not exist.

Peak Performance and Motivation

In a human life, achievement goals are largely shaped between the ages of six and 14. Intrinsically-motivated people have a greater advantage than ego-driven individuals since the intrinsically-motivated person loves what they do and is motivated by their own passion. Self-acceptance is more important than self-esteem. Intrinsically-motivated individuals try to improve their performance because they believe they are competing against themselves and tend to be more task-oriented; their main objective is to constantly improve themselves and be the best they can be. Meanwhile, extrinsically-motivated individuals are more ego-driven and motivated by being better than their competitors.

In the past, peak performance was an untouched avenue of improving sport performance. However, in recent years, the sports community has recognized that mental factors such as confidence, composure, focus, and motivation are highly significant to peak performance, in addition to optimizing resilience and controlling anger, anxiety, frustration, fear, and more. As a result, peak performance coaching has become an emerging practice within the field of psychology and sport coaching.

Peak performance coaches believe that in order for athletes to get the most out of their sport, they must develop a strong mental game to complement their physical talent. Athletes deemed to have a strong mental game have the ability to move on after mistakes, maintain confidence and composure in the face of adversity, and focus on what is needed to execute each task successfully.

Mental skills, just like physical skills, take repetition, practice, and game-time application to develop. Helping athletes and coaches understand the mental barriers that limit performance and how to overcome them is a critical step in the mental training process.

Mental barriers include high expectations, perfectionism, fear of failure, and lack of emotional control and attention focus. Athletes can overcome these barriers through sport-related psychic interventions that aim to enhance confidence, focus, composure, trust, and resilience.

Maslow's hierarchy of needs can be a very good psychology development platform. Maslow's hierarchy of needs is based on five main components: (1) physiological needs, (2) safety needs, (3) love and belonging needs, (4) esteem needs, and (5) self-actualization needs. Its main purpose is to help people determine their sources of motivation and priorities. Athletes can use Maslow's hierarchy of needs to understand their needs, based on importance and priority.

According to Maslow, "People are motivated to achieve their needs; some needs take precedence over others." People's most basic needs are their physiological needs (level 1), like food, shelter, rest, and their need for safety and security (level 2). These needs address physical survival. The third level is the need for belonging and love; for example, relationships and friends. Level four is the need for esteem, like prestige and the feelings of accomplishment. Lastly, at the top of Maslow's hierarchy (level 5) is self-actualization or self-fulfilling needs. This refers to fulfilling one's full potential, and it includes creative needs.

To summarize, satisfying basic needs will be the first thing that motivates our behavior. Once that level is fulfilled, the next component of the pyramid becomes the source of motivation, and so on until we reach the need for fulfilling our potential through activities such as art and athletics—places we can put our performance to the test.

This five-stage model can be divided into "deficiency" needs and "growth" needs. The first four levels are often referred to as deficiency needs, and the top level is known as growth needs.

We must satisfy our lower-level deficit needs before progressing to meet higher-level growth needs. When a deficit need has been met, our activities then become directed towards meeting the next set of needs that we have yet to satisfy. These then become our next immediate prominent needs. When all these "growth" needs have been reasonably satisfied, we may be able to reach the highest level called self-actualization. Every person is capable of and has the desire to move up the hierarchy toward a level of self-actualization. Unfortunately, our progress is often disrupted by failure to meet a lower-level need.

Life experiences, including divorce and the loss of job, for example, may cause an individual to fluctuate between levels of the hierarchy. Therefore, not everyone will move through the hierarchy in the same manner. Many may move back and forth between different types of needs. Understanding needs for motivation and how to boost motivation and meet an athlete's needs are clearly explained through Maslow's hierarchy and provide a smart mental strategy for mental development in peak performance.

As peak performance bases itself on the fact that performance is 90 percent mental, it uses mental coaching and sport psychology as a cornerstone for personal and sport performance. If you are an athlete desiring to perform at peak levels, it is important to pay attention to both the internal and external factors that influence your training and motivation. It is also important to remember that running, jumping, and studying aren't the only factors to improvement in sport performance. What are the philosophical and sociological conditions that influence your mindset? Are your basic needs getting met? Do you have healthy relationships driving your performance? Is your training driven intrinsically (meaning by a motivation to compete with yourself) or extrinsically (meaning by a motivation to be better than others)?

To be good at sports, you do not need to think so deeply about the conscious and unconscious factors influencing your mental idea of performance, excellence, and perfection. But, for the athlete wanting to push limits to the very farthest, it is important to take a much more holistic view of yourself, your relationships with others, and the mindset tools you use to reach full self-actualization and arrive at a state of peak performance in your sport.

About the Author

Tarek Charaf, PhD, is an adviser in international sport development. He has been working on the international Olympic circuit for more than 20 years, being involved in the development of National Olympic Committees, government sports master plans, national strategic development plans, and other areas.

Prior to that, Tarek was an international water polo athlete and is a certified coach in swimming, water polo, golf, snowboarding, and scuba diving. He has done extensive work for various countries and governments, as well as many international sport governing bodies, such as the International Olympic committee (IOC), the International Swimming Federation (FINA), the International Golf Federation (IGF), the European Disabled Golf Association (EDGA), the tennis ATP and WTA tours, the International Ice Hockey Federation/Asian Strategic Planning Group (IIHF/ASPG), and other international organizations.

Tarek is also a renowned peak performance coach. He has developed a unique methodology mixing sports psychology, cognitive behavioral therapy, and mindfulness-based therapy. He holds a PhD in management and sports management, as well as diplomas in sport psychology and cognitive behavioral therapy.

Email: tarek@tarekcharaf.com
LinkedIn: https://www.linkedin.com/in/dr-tarek-charaf-11727a51/

CHAPTER SEVEN

THE 5 TS—YOU SHOULD NOT DO IT ALL BY YOURSELF

By Robert Fegg
National and Olympic Team Coach for Luge
Calgary, Alberta, Canada

The strength of the team is each individual member.
The strength of each member is the team.
—Phil Jackson

Coaches seem to always look for ways to teach the majority of athletes the same thing. This is because they think they don't have enough time to be more individualizing, or they just don't know better. But they find out quickly that things don't always work the same for all.

Over the last two decades of coaching on a development and elite level, I have come to the conclusion that there is one essential thing for each athlete that gives them the chance to perform at their highest level possible. When it comes to a high-performance mindset, there is much more to it than just simply "do this" or "do that." In sport, athletes do have pressure to perform well, but it should come from their own expectation to start with.

It is also easy for everyone, coaches included, to just say that an athlete crumbled under the pressure, or they don't have what it takes. But when you are honest with yourself as a coach, or anybody else involved in sport besides the athlete, are we doing everything needed and possible to set you, as an athlete and human being, up for success? Or do our actions prevent you from succeeding? While having these thoughts over many years, diving into the topic of mindset and mental training more and more, I realized that everyone behind the scenes can do so much more to help an athlete to have the chance to succeed.

Based on this, I came up with an explanation of a method that has worked for me while working with many athletes from different countries, and it has proven to be successful. Granted, it is only one tool in the toolbox, but it is important. I call it the 5 Ts

The 5 Ts are all directly connected with each other, and each one is either an ingredient to the whole or a consequence. The 5 Ts are team, transparency, trust, tenacity, and thriving.

Team

A team is two or more individuals who work together or play on the same side as in a game.

Even though the sport you are practicing or coaching might not be a team sport, very rarely do you work without a team. Your sport association, your coaches, your support staff—they all are part of it. And even though you are the one who has to perform in the field of play, your team's job should be to prepare you the best they can.

How often do you feel the pressure of something you have no or barely any influence in? Your organisation is not as organized as they should be? Not understood decisions weigh heavy on you? You feel like you're being treated unfairly? Or everything is just very confusing and just the thought of it keeps you away from doing what you love doing in the first place? I know those feelings all too well from back then when I was an athlete.

The team surrounding you is the foundation of your success. We, as your team, must make sure that we do a better job in keeping those thoughts away from you as much as possible. We have to give you the feeling that you are being heard, understood, and that you can come anytime with possible questions and suggestions. It is our job to create an environment in which you can put all your energy and motivation into areas that are important for your success and that you can influence. The fact that you invest your time and energy, more than necessary, into things that are not in your "job description" as an athlete has turned out to be very counterproductive many times in the past. It can be very exhausting, to say the least. Your team should take care of that.

Transparency

Transparency is an approach to communicating and forming relationships that emphasize being direct with people in your workplace.

The most important ingredient for building your ideal environment is transparency. Coaches must be clear with the direction they are going in terms of athletes. Coaches should include athletes when possible. It is important that the athlete's opinion is being heard, or at least that they are being kept in the loop as much as possible. A coach's holding back of important information results in a lack of clarity in the athlete and is grounds for unnecessary discussions or even accusations in the future.

Transparency also sends a message. It is a sign of honesty and trust, and that there is nothing to hide. And that goes both ways. It is forming the relationship between you and your team based on trust. Many things an organisation and coaches are dealing with is of a political nature. There will always be some athletes who don't make the team or do not feel treated fairly. But when the communication about the important developments within the organisation, especially the ones that are directly connected with your success as an athlete, is clear and complete, that will give you more certainty that things have gone right.

For me, as a coach, communication is the most important tool I have. It is my way of giving you the confidence that you know what you need to know to do your job. You need to know how to get where you want to go, but also what could be in our way. That is me preparing you for every possible outcome. And that creates trust.

Trust

Trust is a firm belief in the reliability, truth, ability, or strength of someone or something.

"Teamwork makes the dream work," but to create this picture, it involves a lot of work on relationships. One must be transparent with others, and everyone involved has to understand that we are chasing the same dream or the same goal. While building these relationships, we will learn to trust and be able to count on one another. Again, that goes both ways. I want you to trust me as your coach that I always create a fair play environment and give you the chance to perform the best you can without holding you back. At the same time, I want to be able to trust you that you will do whatever it takes to get there as well. Being able to rely on one another forms a team that will be hard to break. Especially in times of failure (and I want you to fail often so you can come out stronger on the other side), the trusted bond between coaches and athletes is the strongest weapon, if used correctly.

The comfort of trust, to be able to discuss any unclarities, is priceless. Often, many things are left behind and not being dealt with because the athlete "doesn't want to be labelled as a problem case, troublemaker" or even fears repercussions. Honest conversations are only possible in a healthy environment, where everyone involved knows their place and rights. And that is only possible with trust.

Tenacity

Tenacity is the quality or fact of being very determined; determination.

The direct result of working in a relationship between coaches and athletes is the level of motivation to continuously give higher effort for a longer period of time. The determination to achieve your goal is higher when you know that you and your team are working towards the same goal, less doubts are present, and you can focus more on things that you can directly influence. You won't have the feeling that you must question everything or that there are unfair motives in play. With this extra boost of trust and confidence that you have built up with your team, your firmness of purpose is channelled towards you, and you will feel more joy in pursuing your daily goals. You know that your coaches will do everything necessary on their end and you don't have to worry about it. But at the same time, you have the comfort to come and ask, to discuss matters when needed or to just simply vent (also an important tool, by the way). With your team having your back, failing will turn more often from being something horrible into something positive, a learning experience and just a step along the way. Every little success on this path will turn into proof that things are going the right way.

A beautiful side effect is that the same goes for your coaches. Their determination is also highly affected by the trust of your relationship. It is a win-win situation, and it is way more fun when all parties involved work together and not against each other.

Thriving

Thriving is a condition beyond mere survival, implying growth and a positive development.

Whenever I have gotten to the point where I was able to form a good team around my athletes and established a trustful relationship with and amongst them, many things started to flourish.

The simple interactions during training sessions became joyful, athletes wanted to be more engaged in training, they started to ask questions in a way where the coaches didn't feel offended, and communication took a turn for the better.

Athletes and coaches continued their communication after a training session to come up with new ideas, or just discuss a topic related to the sport, or even not related to their sport. The increase of trust and joy of everyone doing their "work" was substantial. Doing things, changing training methods, bringing up ideas, and discussing them turned into a fun activity. And let me tell you, it is productive.

To analyze failure, to take the good from it and move on, has never been an easy task. Not for the athlete to accept failure, nor for the coach to talk about it. And it still isn't, but it is not a burden anymore. It is a part of the road to the goal. Together we can move mountains, even if they are small at first.

Thriving is a consequence of the first four Ts. It cannot be avoided. Obviously, it does not always result in you winning the Olympic gold medal, but you will thrive in many other ways as well. Your relationships to peers, your outlook on working towards your goals, your self-confidence, your ability to trust other people, and much more.

Effect of Implementing the 5 Ts

Working closely together with athletes can create uncomfortable situations for your coaches. Therefore, knowing your place is very important. Your coaches are your team, they will work for you relentlessly and will go the extra mile, if they are good coaches. Especially when you are able to build a relationship based on trust with one another. The important thing not to forget is that they are still your coaches, not necessarily your friends. There might be a time when they have to make decisions that are not in your favour. Therefore, it is important for coaches to set boundaries and rules.

That being said, with covering the 5 Ts, everyone knows what is on the line and also is aware of all possible outcomes. The team will work to the best of their abilities to create a fair field of play (coaches) and perform the best possible when it really counts (athletes).

You, as an athlete, feel a lot of pressure to perform, no matter what. During your career, you will be provided many tools for conquering your mind and setting yourself up for success. Often people forget that there is the other side of mental pressure that is hindering you from performing. This is a pressure that does not have to weigh on your shoulders as an athlete. I see it as the duty of me, as a coach, to build a foundation with a team that can minimize this kind of pressure laid upon you.

You will perform the best if you can train and perform in an environment where you don't have to occupy your mind with things that are not relevant while executing your sport. Irrelevant issues that should not be the concern of athletes includes the following:

- Does my coach like the other team members better than me?
- Will I be cut from the team if I say something?
- Are they really caring about what I am doing here?
- Is my coach giving me the right information?
- And so many more...

There are so many thoughts that can hinder you from performing to the best of your capabilities and keep you from developing yourself to the highest level possible. It is on your team surrounding you to provide you with enough transparency and information, support, and commitment to avoid those thoughts or doubts as much as possible.

Because, guess what? When you are at the start of the Olympic Games (or any other event that is your goal to win a medal at), you will feel enough pressure to perform well that there is no need or place for such pressure that could have been avoided in the first place or can be carried by one of your team members.

When I worked in South Korea between 2014 and 2018, leading up to their home Olympic Winter Games in Pyeongchang, my colleague and I were faced with the challenge of being provided athletes who were absolute beginners in 2014. We had the time frame of four years to create Olympic athletes out of them in luge, a sport that normally requires eight to 12 years of experience to become competitive. Team South Korea finished with three top-10 finishes in luge at the Olympic Games in 2018.

While writing this chapter, I reached out to my former athletes JinYong Park and Myung Jung Cho who finished ninth in the double seater discipline in 2018. I asked them what they thought were the reasons that they became so successful in such a short period of time. Their answers were astonishing, even to me.

JinYong Park responded, "The mental part was very difficult, but it was achieved because the faith and the goal of the coaches and athletes became one."

Myung Jung Cho told me, "Everything was well prepared for the Games. We had a clear goal in the preparation process, and having a good relationship between the players and coaches was a great help in preparing for the Games. Mentally, it is easier when you are well prepared. A trusting relationship with your partner and coaches, along with overcoming anxiety with a lot of training and competitions, creates a strong mentality."

Drawing from their experience as athletes and coupling that with my experience as a coach, I'll end by simply saying that to reach levels of peak performance in sport—you are not alone, and you don't have to do it all by yourself!

About the Author

Robert Fegg is a successful coach in the sport of luge. He has coached on several levels with athletes on the development team, national team, and Olympic team over the past 20 years. Coaching has been in Robert's blood since he wrapped up an eight-year career sliding on the German National Team in 2002. He cut his teeth into the coaching ranks the following year when he became the assistant coach of the Canadian Luge Team. With coaching stints in Canada from 2002 to 2014 (Olympic Games Torino 2006 and Vancouver 2010), South Korea from 2014 to 2018 (Pyeongchang 2018), the USA from 2018 to 2022 (Beijing 2022), and now back in Canada as the head coach, Robert collected a wealth of knowledge from around the globe. Robert is committed to developing an athlete-centred program where athletes can develop on and off the ice.

Email: rfegg.luge@gmail.com
LinkedIn: www.linkedin.com/in/robert-fegg-22910535/

CHAPTER EIGHT
PEAK PREPARATION

By Sacha Fulton, PhD
Sport Scientist, Athlete Preparation Specialist
Perth, Australia

It has been some time since I last entered HBF Stadium in Perth, Western Australia. Yet, as I descend the ramp to the gymnasium, I am hit with nostalgia. An all too familiar smell and feel arise, which, until now, has been impossible to describe. In its rawness, the scent is stuffy, sweaty, chalky, and salty. The scent has been years in the making, but it is not just time. Hundreds of thousands of minutes, yes, but it is more than that. It is hundreds and thousands of skills, heart beats, blisters, tears, injuries, falls, hugs, and high fives. Here bodies were pushed and spirits were lifted in the pursuit of dreams. Commonwealth and Olympic medallists and World Champions were created in this gymnasium. Millions of moments are felt and remembered in this scent that has hit me for the thousandth time, but that has only been defined now. It is the scent of preparation.

Gymnastics is just one sport I have had the pleasure of working in during my career as a sports scientist. I have travelled nationally and internationally with teams and with some of the world's best athletes. I have watched hundreds of training sessions, and I have watched performance at its finest. I can conclude that peak performance is not possible without peak preparation, and elite athletes prepare better than anyone else on the planet.

My "peak preparation" is about unlocking potential and cultivating greatness for individuals to achieve their true potential. I believe that success is what happens when peak preparation meets knowledge. "Peak preparation" was born somewhere along the Camino de Santiago as I hiked 1,700 kilometers across France and Spain. When I boarded a plane to France in 2018 to set off on the Camino with nothing but an eight-kilogram backpack, I had never heard of the Camino de Santiago. I was running away from Australia and from a recent personal tragedy. Armed with nothing more than a sense of adventure and nothing to lose, I would simply follow the red-and-white markers along "the way" and find accommodation when I got tired. I averaged 28 kilometers a day, and I suffered in ways I have never suffered before—physically, mentally, emotionally, and spiritually. I learnt many things on "the way", but what I really learnt is this. Performance is not something you deserve. Performance cannot come before preparation. Peak performance takes time, and peak preparation takes longer.

Preparation for athletes is not as simple as it might seem. Preparation is not just about eating your greens, getting eight hours of sleep a night, and turning up to practice. Preparation is more than just repeating a skill a million times until it can be performed without thinking.

Preparation is calculated, deliberate, and planned. Preparation is the consummate sum of the body, mind, and spirit. Preparation is about competence, confidence, connections, character, and caring. Preparation is a process. The definition of preparation is "the process of getting ready for some occasion". When we talk about preparation and how it relates to human beings, we are dealing with something entirely different. Ever since people learned to write, we've documented how special we are. The philosopher Aristotle marked out our differences over 2,000 years ago. We are "rational animals", pursuing knowledge for its own sake. We live by art and reasoning, he wrote. Through art, our language-learning abilities were gradually developed and "switched on".

In the same way that birds developed feathers before they could fly, human beings had the mental tools for complex language before we developed it. As human beings, we tell stories, we dream, we imagine things about ourselves and others, and we spend a great deal of time thinking about the future and analysing the past. Humans are complex beings, and elite athletes are finely tuned machines, the very best of the best. Unlike a finely tuned computer system, however, we cannot just "input" the end result and hope for the best. In the world of elite sport, athletes constantly strive to break records and achieve what no other human being has achieved. We set ridiculously high benchmarks, such as breaking the four-minute mile barrier and breaking the two-hour marathon barrier. The latter is a feat that has only been achieved by one man, Eluid Kipchoge in very recent years. The thing is, that these end results roll off the tongue so seamlessly that we are forgiven for forgetting the "inputs" required to achieve them. Hundreds of thousands of minutes, yes, but it is more than that.

Elite athletes are not just athletically gifted. It is hundreds and thousands of skills, heartbeats, blisters, tears, hugs, injuries, falls, and high fives. It is hundreds of thousands of minutes of "competence", "confidence", "connections", "character", and "caring" (Lerner, et al., 2005). Once developed as the 5 Cs of positive youth development, I have taken this concept and made it my own. I call it the 5 Cs of "peak athletic preparation".

My matrix for peak preparation, therefore, looks like this:

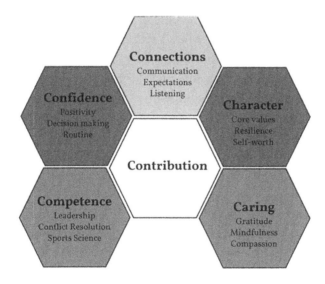

Let's pull this matrix apart and have a look at each of the 5 Cs in more detail.

Competence—*Leadership, Conflict Resolution, Sports Science*

Competence can be defined as "successful and efficient accomplishment through knowledge and learning". Elite athletes are hungry for knowledge and hungry to learn. In an elite athletic space competence involves leadership, conflict resolution, and sports science. Athletes who have knowledge in these key areas will be well on their way to achieving competence and one step closer to being optimally prepared.

The leadership part of competence is the ability to inspire and influence, to motivate and cultivate change. In the words of Henry Kissinger, "The task of the leader is to get his people from where they are to where they have not been". One elite athlete who has recently shown incredible leadership is Eileen Gu, a Chinese, American-born freestyle skier and two-time Olympic gold medallist. Gu opted to represent her birth mother's home country of China to influence more people. Gu claimed she had achieved success even before she claimed her first medal at the recent winter Olympic Games in Beijing, that is, to help inspire young girls in China to compete in skiing.

The conflict resolution aspect of competence can often feel uncomfortable; however, it is essential for success and good relationships. Business leader Orrin Woodward describes conflict simply, "Conflict is like a fire. Easy to snuff out when small but nearly impossible to handle when not dealt with quickly." Not addressing conflict immediately and directly isn't a good plan if you want to maintain relationships and success. "Bo" Hanson is a four-time Australian Olympian in rowing and a three-time Olympic medallist. Bo was part of that Olympic final, which saw just 1.37 seconds separate all podium finishers including five-time Olympic gold medallist Sir Steven Redgrave. No stranger to conflict within teams, Hanson doesn't see conflict as the downfall of a team or even a crisis, but instead as a by-product of the diversity within a successful team.

The sports science part of competence is the study of the long- and short-term effects of training and conditions on athletes. A sports scientist optimises human potential and sporting performance using scientific knowledge, methods, and applications. A sports scientist evaluates the research and advises on the technical and practical aspects of training, injury prevention, technique, nutritional supplements, and performance and recovery practices. The foundations of sports science, including anatomy, physiology, psychology, biomechanics motor control, and testing prescription, are at the heart of human optimisation on all levels. Listening to the advice of sport science, swimmer Michael Phelps holds the all-time records for Olympic gold medals, Olympic gold medals in individual events, and Olympic medals in individual events. Phelps has said that he would sleep at least eight hours per night, and take a two- to three-hour nap during the day. "Sleeping is a crucial part of my everyday life."

Confidence—*Positivity, Decision Making, Routine*

Confidence can be defined as a "clear-headed feeling of self-assurance from an appreciation of one's own abilities or qualities." Confidence involves positivity, decision making, and routine. Athletes who are positive, who make good decisions, and who follow a daily routine are generally well on their way to achieving confidence and are, thus, one step closer to being optimally prepared. The tendency to be positive or optimistic in attitude goes hand in hand with sport. Elite athletes compete to be the best, to come first, to break records, and to win medals. Achievement is essentially impossible if you don't have a positive mindset and don't believe you can win.

Many athletes recall previous sporting success as a way of staying positive under pressure, or they arm themselves with self-affirmations to bring about a positive mindset in times of stress. Muhammad Ali, nicknamed The Greatest, is widely regarded as one of the most significant and celebrated sports figures of the 20th century. Frequently ranked as the greatest heavyweight boxer of all time, Ali was known for his positivity and belief, "'I am the greatest'. I said that before I even knew I was".

In sport, the decision-making process often occurs in milliseconds. These are those breath-taking decisions that leave spectators in awe. Breath-taking, yes, but unbelievable, no. Such decisions have been practiced over and over again in training and in competition. They have not occurred out of thin air. They have been tried and tested and failed and refined and tried again hundreds of thousands of times so that when it comes to crunch time, with a fraction of luck on their side, a breath-taking play is what spectators see. Decision-making is closely linked to problem solving. So, by taking responsibility, understanding the reason a decision was made, unpacking the process, and identifying areas for targeted practice, future decisions can be improved. Excellent decision-making results from ongoing practice in the training environment, where athletes can refine and hone their ability, weigh their options, make decisions, and make mistakes. Decision-making improves when athletes are *consciously constructively debriefed*, so mistakes don't reoccur in the future, and brilliant play is replicated.

Routines are one of the most important aspects of sport that athletes can develop to improve their training and competitive performances. There is no world-class athlete in any sport who does not use routines as part of competitive preparations. The fundamental value of routines is that they ensure total preparation in athletes' efforts. Routines enable athletes to be completely physically, technically, tactically, and mentally ready to perform their best. If athletes can reduce the things that can go wrong and be prepared for those things that do, they'll be better able to stay focused and relaxed before and during competition.

Connections—*Communication, Expectations, Listening*

Connections can be defined as "the linking together of two or more people". Connections on and off the sporting field are important for humans as we are innately social beings. We like to be surrounded by friends, and we like to share our personal experiences with others. Connections involve communication, expectations, and listening. Athletes who have knowledge in these key areas are well on their way to achieving connections and one step closer to being optimally prepared.

Communication is the foundation upon which a coach builds their team. In the words of James Hume, an author and former presidential speechwriter, "The art of communication is the language of leadership". Effective communication is often cited as the critical element of success in athletic teams. Team members must learn how to communicate with each other, both on and off the playing field, so they can become one cohesive unit and ultimately increase their chance of success. Communication from the coach must be articulated in a fashion that the athletes not only hear, but instantly understand. Joe Torre, former Major League Baseball manager who led the New York Yankees to four World Series titles, emphasized, "Communication is the key to trust, and trust is the key to teamwork".

Dealing with high expectations is almost inevitable when athletes are striving for peak preparation. Athletes need to be aware and educate themselves on how to deal with these expectations. I remember growing up with the quote, "Shoot for the moon. Even if you miss, you'll land among the stars". Unfortunately, athletes with this mentality heap excessive demands upon themselves, believing this method will result in personal best or optimal performances, which rarely occur. When expectations are high, so is the pressure to meet those expectations.

Nathan Wei Chen, the 2022 American Olympic figure skating champion, is no stranger to high expectations. At only 22 years of age, he is the only man in history to land five quads in an Olympic final. Despite his love for the sport, he has had to learn to deal with stress, nerves, and the inevitable unknown that comes with being at the top. "It's easy to get stuck thinking about what could go wrong", he says. So, instead of worrying about not landing a jump, Chen has learned to trust his talents and hard work. "Spending so much time training, honing our craft, it would be a disservice if we don't trust ourselves", he commented. These days, he prefers to focus on "having as much fun on the ice as possible".

"Listening is the language of leadership". When we take time to listen to another, in depth, until they feel understood, we are communicating to them their worth and their potential. Good listeners strive to fully understand what others want to communicate. Active listeners show curiosity by interpreting verbal messages and nonverbal cues, like tone of voice, facial expressions, and physical posture, and they ask questions. Great athletes listen intently to gain new perspectives and new insights. They listen to their coaches and support staff. They listen to their teammates, opponents, and fans. Listening to others enables athletes to solve problems and see new opportunities.

Take Michael Phelps, considered to be the greatest Olympic swimmer of all time. As a child, Phelps suffered from ADHD. People with ADHD suffer from restlessness, impulsiveness, and very short attention spans. However, they also have an incredible capacity to remain hyper-focused on an activity they are passionate about. Phelps was able to use this with enormous success. By channelling his energy, listening, and focus, he exploited the positive side of ADHD.

Character—*Core Values, Resilience, Self-Worth*

Character can be defined as "the mental and moral qualities distinctive to an individual". Athletes who succeed are the ones that have done so by remaining true to who they are. Their pursuit to be the best hasn't come at the cost of changing who they are. Character involves core values, resilience, and self-worth. Athletes who know their character and self-worth are those who are one step closer to being optimally prepared. Core values are the guideposts for your actions and decisions. Roger Federer's hard work and single-minded devotion to tennis is so often hidden from public view, and his unique brand of magic on the court can fool the casual viewer into thinking it is "effortless" or just "natural talent". Federer's success is very much linked to his core values and how he embodies these on a daily basis.

Resilience is "the capacity of a dynamic system to adapt successfully to challenges that threaten the function, survival, or future development of the system". In short, resilience is the capacity to recover quickly from difficulties. Take the story of Kieran Behan OLY, an Irish artistic gymnast, who represents Ireland internationally. At the age of 10 and following the removal of a cancerous tumour from his thigh, Kieran was told that he would never walk again and was confined to a wheelchair. Up to then, he had been crazy about gymnastics and was determined to become an Olympic champion. Kieran was adamant he was going to defy the odds and started the long road to recovery. Within just a few months of returning to the gym, he slipped from the high bar and sustained a terrible head injury. He experienced frequent blackouts and missed a whole year at school. However, this still did not deter him. He had to retrain his brain to return to school and regain his coordination to return to the gym. It then took him three years to get back to where he had been before snapping his knee just after he had been selected for the European Championships. He never gave up and succeeded in qualifying for the 2012 London Olympics.

Self-worth can be defined as "the internal sense of being good enough and worthy of love and belonging from others". For an athlete to succeed, they have to be able to identify their positive traits and see these, irrespective of performance. For many athletes, performance is strongly tied to feelings of self-worth. Multiple instances of high-level success in an athlete's career can offset the negative impact of one or two losses. However, multiple negative instances can impact deeply on feelings of self-worth. It takes a very grounded athlete to be able to separate feelings of self-worth from being worthy and feelings of self-worth from performance.

Dylan Alcott, AO is an Australian former wheelchair tennis and basketball player. Long before he was an award-winning Paralympian and celebrated disability advocate, Alcott was a child filled with self-hatred and doubt. This year, the tennis star made history by becoming the first Australian of the Year with a physical disability. The seven-time Australian Open champion has been very open with sharing what was vital in transforming his perspective that he could have a fulfilling life, saying, "I had the best friends and family who told me I was worthy, and I was allowed to be loved". Alcott said as soon as he became proud of his disability, everyone around him did too.

Caring—*Gratitude, Mindfulness, Compassion*

The final C on my matrix of peak athletic preparation is caring. Caring can be defined as "actively displaying kindness and concern for others". Caring involves gratitude, mindfulness, and compassion. Athletes who understand and incorporate these key areas of caring into their lives are one step closer to being optimally prepared.

Gratitude is the quality of being thankful; it is readiness to show appreciation for and to return kindness. At its most basic, practicing gratitude can start to reorganize our mental focus. Practicing gratitude increases happiness and creates a shift away from resentment, jealousy, and other negative emotions. Individuals who regularly practice gratitude sleep better, express more compassion, feel more alive, have stronger immune systems, and have a more positive outlook. Gratitude is also related to higher levels of optimism, life satisfaction, and well-being, and a greater likelihood of engaging in enriching behaviour. Gratitude helps us to focus on what really matters and is the foundation of sportsmanship.

Mindfulness is the practice of purposely bringing your attention in the present moment without evaluation, and it can be developed through meditation. Mindfulness and meditation are all about training and soothing the mind, entering a freedom and self-awareness mode that induces relaxation, joy, patience, emotional balance, and love.

Surfing is a great example of a sport where athletes have adopted mindfulness and meditation as a way of perfecting their craft. Surfers are always looking to achieve perfect synchronicity—with nature, the ocean, and the waves. Surfers of all levels constantly need to build concentration, focus, and attention so that they are in tune with the elements and, most of all, themselves. Robert Kelly Slater, an American professional surfer, is best known for being crowned World Surf League champion a record 11 times. Slater is widely regarded as the greatest surfer of all time and is famously quoted for saying, "It's all about where your mind's at." Learning to develop a practice of mindful awareness helps athletes reach their optimal potential under pressure in competition.

Compassion is what helps you overcome the impulse to judge another harshly. You put yourself in their shoes and you're open to what they have to say and slow to assume they're in the wrong. You want to understand them more than you want to be right. If you were to cultivate a compassion code for yourself, it might look something like this: "I make compassion the foundation of my behavior and thoughts toward others". After a very close and intense 2005 Ashes cricket match between England and Australia, England came out in an extremely narrow two-run victory. While the crowd and team all leapt to their feet in celebration, Freddie Flintoff had spotted Australian player Brett Lee slumped over in defeat, and, instead of immediately joining his own team to celebrate, walked over and offered a consoling handshake. This gentle act of sportsmanship has now become one of the most famous sporting photographs of all time, and this seemingly small gesture had a massive impact on the players and those that witnessed it.

When I first registered my business name, Peak Preparation, people questioned. I was a sports scientist who had been working with Olympic and Paralympic athletes for many years. Surely with my background and skill set my business name should be Peak Performance. I believe that success is what happens when preparation meets knowledge. Performance can only be achieved once preparation and knowledge have been achieved. Performance cannot come without preparation. My purpose is to unlock possibility and cultivate greatness for individuals to achieve their full potential. I can't guarantee performance, but I can guarantee that if you get up in the morning, put your shoes on, and follow the 5 Cs of "peak athletic preparation", you will reach your destination.

About the Author

Dr. Sacha Fulton successfully secured a sports-based PhD scholarship in 2005 with Swimming Australia and the Australian Institute of Sport. Her PhD was titled "Performance Characteristics of Paralympic Swimmers". Concurrently, Sacha was appointed as physiologist for the Australian Paralympic Swimming team.

Sacha worked with the team in a professional capacity up until 2013 and accompanied them to the Beijing Paralympic Games in 2008 and the London Paralympic Games in 2012. In 2009, after the successful submission of her PhD, Sacha gained employment at the Western Australian Institute of Sport. She worked with the institute for over nine years, assisting in the athletic improvement of Olympic and aspiring Olympic hopefuls.

In 2018, Sacha established her own sports science consulting business in Perth, Western Australia. Sacha is passionate about sport and helping individuals unlock their potential and reach their goals. Sacha is equally passionate about life, driven to embark on challenges and adventures and committed to her own personal and professional growth.

Email: sacha@peakpreparation.com.au
Website: www.peakpreparation.com.au

CHAPTER NINE
IRON SHARPENS IRON

By Ryne Glazier
Professional Strength and Conditioning Coach
Dallas, Texas

You become like the five people you spend the most time with. Choose carefully.
—Jim Rohn

The relationship between the sports we play and the life we live are parallel. Our pregame routines mirror our morning routines. The way we outline and attack each competition resembles the way we intentionally plan the moves of our everyday life. Even our post-game recovery emulates the way we relax and refresh after each day we live. It's important to note that some days require more recovery than others. Then there is also the fact that most people want to be on the best sports teams and win just as most people want to go to the best schools to work the highest jobs in the most successful companies. When we take a step back and look at the big picture, both of everyday life and competitive sports, the ones who are the most successful in both have one very important thing in common—culture.

Culture, by definition, is the normal practices, beliefs, social forms, and material traits shared by a group of people in a particular place or time. The New Zealand All Blacks rugby dynasty, the Montreal Canadians in the 1970s, the Chicago Bulls in the 1990s, and even the New England Patriots in the early 2000s—all these organizations are examples that can attribute their success to the culture each group built behind the scenes and in front of the crowds.

Whether we saw it during the season, in the postseason documentary, or not at all, these groups of athletes came together and laid out an intricate plan to win multiple years in a short period of time.

Now, if you are an athlete, you coach athletes, or you even just grew up a fan of sports, I bet you were already familiar with these teams. I know we all watched *The Last Dance* on Netflix in 2020 because, let's be honest, with live sports at a halt, this was the closest a sports fan could get to an actual game. I bet you're thinking to yourself that these teams were successful because they had some of the best players in the world, some even multiple great players. And that is 100 percent correct! Michael Jordan had Scottie Pippen, Denis Rodman, and Steve Kerr, and was led by the great Phil Jackson. The Patriots had Bill Belichick lead players like Drew Bledsoe, Tom Brady, Kevin Faulk, Rob Gronkowski, and many others that contributed to their winning seasons the last 20 years. So, yes, I agree. These teams had some of the best players of their time, but it is how those players built up and led their other teammates that really contributed to their winning culture.

Now these examples of successful organizations are cool and all, but how does this apply to an athlete, coach, or human individual like yourself? Well, let's take Michael Jordan and the 1990 Chicago Bulls. Michael was known for being hard on teammates in practices, and in the documentary, *The Last Dance*, we see this up close. Michael would force his teammates to his level, sometimes in unruly but passionate ways. He wanted to be able to depend on the guys around him when the game got tough, and the best way he could build trust with his teammates was by molding them into fierce competitors at practice, subsequently making them better basketball players overall. His teammates may have hated him in the process, but at the end of the day, that's the player they wanted on their team. Someone to push the pace, force them to essentially level up their work capacity and skills to compete at their highest caliber. Wouldn't you want to consistently perform as the highest caliber player on your team, especially if it is Michael Jordan, arguably one of the best players to ever play basketball?

Exactly my point. This is the mindset you need to take and apply into your own life. You become who you surround yourself with. That is true in sports. That is true in business. That is true in life. When it comes down to the nitty gritty of it, look around at the people you train with, the people you work with, and the people you choose to keep in your day-to-day life. The people you train with will dictate how hard you work, day in and day out. The people you work with will determine how much effort you put in and will contribute to the success you earn. The people you have around you in your daily life will influence all the habits you create. All these people ultimately reflect how you respond to both adversity and accomplishment, so it is important to choose the right influences to surround yourself with that are aligned with your goals.

This starts with YOU. As an athlete or coach, you must look within and ask yourself two very important questions. One, what is your number one goal right now? And two, are the people you surround yourself with going to help you reach that goal? These are the two questions I have broken it down to for myself in every new stage of life I start. It has really let me take a step back, assess my situation and the environment I am in, and then change what I need.

For example, I have worked as a strength and conditioning coach for the last seven years. My long-term goal is to own my own gym and be well-known in my community as a hard-working coach who emphasizes a competitive and team-centered culture that can provide results. I also value a growth mindset and prioritize continuing education. My number one goal right now is to be in a leadership position in a gym focused on my core values, which I have accomplished.

How did I do that? I was very fortunate to have worked for Ben Prentiss, a very well-known strength and conditioning coach, early on in my career. Ben works with many Olympic, professional, collegiate, and elite-level youth athletes in southern Connecticut (he is currently the Strength and Conditioning Coordinator for the New York Rangers). It was through him that I discerned the type of coach I wanted to be, learned about the kind of research and education I wanted to prioritize and implement into my coaching, and observed how to be a compassionate samurai.

I was lucky to get opportunities through him to meet other successful coaches in the college and private setting as well as work the New York Rangers' development and training camp. This allowed me to create relationships within the industry as well as gain incredible experience as I progressed forward in my career. When I moved back to Texas in 2021, Ben's experience and guidance gave me a good foundation to use when looking for the right gym that lined up with my core values to continue my coaching journey.

This great gym has allowed me to continue to surround myself with other coaches that have more knowledge and experience to learn from and connect with. Being in an environment where coaches are constantly learning and wanting to be on the forefront of science is contagious. From a young age, I never liked being the best on the team or the smartest in the room. I would get too comfortable and simply not improve. To become great and enhance your craft, you need to surround yourself with those who are great. Usually that requires you to set aside your ego and start from the bottom. The good news is that the only way from there is up. Like the Chicago Bulls in the 1990s, I put myself in roles and situations that challenge and push me out of my comfort zone to be a better coach, and person, than I was yesterday … just not by Michael Jordan.

Once you have figured out those two things, your current goal and environment, the next question you need to ask yourself is "What would be a perfect environment to achieve my goal?" In essence, you want to build your dream culture for your life. What would your habits be? Who would you want to learn from? Who would you want to help keep you accountable? Questions like these are a good foundation to build from when deciding who you want to become to achieve your goals because when it really comes down to it, you probably won't be doing it alone. Who are going to be your teammates helping you rise up?

As great as Michael Jordan was, he absolutely did not win all those games alone. He had Scottie Pippen who could fill in anywhere on the court, Denis Rodman who was a defensive all-star and could rebound the ball from anywhere, and coach Phil Jackson whose 11 NBA championships speak for themselves. Michael had the right help at the right time, and so should you. You should emphasize building the right people around you that stay in line with your goals, and more importantly, your values.

Do you have certain friends that spend money when you're trying to save, or are out partying every weekend when you're trying to get extra work done? Do you have teammates that don't want to give it their all every day? Do you have coaches that don't hold you or the team accountable? Maybe it's time to minimize the amount of time you spend around these people. Be greedy with your time and the amount of access people have to you. Find friends who understand your goals and are on the same page as you. Find teammates that are going to push you, challenge you in a positive way. Find a coach who demands your very best every day and will invest in you. Find people who believe in you. FIND PEOPLE WHO MOTIVATE YOU.

The cool thing about today's world is that those people do not have to be geographically close to you. With the click of a button, you can find anything and everything you need on the internet. When I was 16, the sport I prioritized was hockey. I lived and breathed it since I was four. My goal each year was to play on the highest-level team that was offered in our area. After not making that team a couple years in a row, I looked myself in the mirror and asked, "Am I doing everything I can, on and off the ice, to make that team?" The short answer was no. Don't get me wrong, I was going to the offseason camp three times a week and playing weekly competitive games, but that's what everyone else was doing too. So, by default, without me even realizing it, that was the bare minimum.

So, knowing what my goal was, I searched the internet for what pro hockey players did in their offseason. This led me to copious amounts of NHL offseason videos where guys were working out multiple times a week, shooting hundreds of pucks, and talked about their nutrition. There were even thousands of videos of skating, stickhandling, and shooting drills. It was basically a video encyclopedia for hockey training. The next day I asked my parents for a gym membership, a hockey net and pucks, and for more carbs and protein at meals. Thankfully they obliged and for that whole summer, I was either working out like Martin St. Louis or shooting pucks like Sydney Crosby (my parents garage door still has the puck marks). After the countless hours of training, shooting, and learning from pro hockey sources (via the internet), the next year I was playing at the level of hockey I'd aspired to the previous years. Having the right influences, whether you know them personally or not, can have a huge impact on the way you achieve your goal.

The final step in creating a successful culture in your life is to take action. As Shia LeBeouf said, "Go out there and do it!" What it comes down to is finding people who motivate you to be better. Start hanging out with the most skilled player on your team and find out what kind of drills they do in their spare time. Sit next to the strongest teammate in your locker room and ask if you can work out with them sometime. Take time to meet with your coaches to ask for feedback on your game and what you can improve. Research and find people who have been successful in your field and ask them to mentor you. Read books that help open your views to different ways to attack and achieve your goals. Ask for help. The key is to act on your intentions and not settle for people who don't fit into your goals. The choice on who you surround yourself with and if you want to be successful is ultimately in your hands.

When you surround yourself with people who are smarter than you, have more experience than you, and have succeeded in what you want to do, that is how you will get better. In the end, mindset is contagious. Ambition is contagious. Success is contagious. You need the right like-minded people around you to challenge you to grow. You need to create the culture in your life that fits your goals in order to be successful. Iron sharpens iron, as man sharpens another.

About the Author

Ryne Glazier is a professional strength and conditioning coach who currently works with athletes and the general population in Dallas, Texas. His professional experience measures seven years working with Olympic, professional, collegiate, and youth athletes in the collegiate and private sector. Ryne completed his bachelor's degree at Xavier University in Cincinnati, Ohio, and his master's degree at Merrimack College in North Andover, Massachusetts. In his spare time, Ryne continues to educate himself in the field and coaches youth hockey in the Dallas Area.

Email: glazierr93@gmail.com

CHAPTER TEN
FIND THE PURPOSE BEHIND PEAK PERFORMANCE

By Jonathan Harris-Wright
Head of Performance Services, Athletic Performance
Greystones, Ireland

He who has a why to live for can bear almost any how.
—Friedrich Nietzsche

In this chapter we will discuss some of the steps used to achieve peak performance with elite athletes. Throughout, specific examples will reference the physical development of those athletes through the real-world application of a strength and power programme used to achieve physical peak performance. However, it is important to understand that the principles discussed in the chapter are not unique to optimising the physical performance of elite athletes in the quest to achieve peak performance. Rather, the principles and examples discussed underpin any high-performing individual or organisation across a multitude of sectors, as these underpinning principles provide the foundations for achieving peak performance. As suggested by Tom Robbins, "Success leaves clues," so regardless of what industry you work in, the principles of peak performance remain the same.

Principles and Values

Having the ability to be consistent over time in ever-changing situations can prove challenging. Therefore, having clarity of your underpinning principles and values are imperative for success over time while dealing with changes in team members and even succeeding in different environments and cultures. Friedrich Nietzsche's quote, "He who has a why to live for can bear almost any how," helps sum up this point well. This principle is something that underpins any successful strength and power programme, project, or business idea, and has allowed many athletes and entrepreneurs to achieve peak performance across a multitude of teams and cultures.

Having the ability to first understand our own principles and values is crucial in achieving peak performance, and these values and principles provide the road map at every crossroads on that journey. Without a clear understanding of our underpinning values and principles we can adopt a short-term mindset in our daily decision-making process, which may not align with what is best for the long-term vision. We are faced with daily challenges and decisions, which can have short-term outcomes that may be beneficial in the moment but may not align with the long-term vision. An example of this is when physically preparing elite athletes for competition, it is not uncommon for them to have a slight injury or movement limitation. With a short-term-focused decision-making process, it may be decided the athlete has a rest day and does not do any training at all, which, on the face of it, makes sense to allow them to recover. However, if we look at the situation with a long-term perspective and keep the vision in mind for achieving sustained peak performance, we may decide to look for modified or alternative ways they can train, which will not impact the injury but will allow them to continue to work towards the vision. This long-term mindset creates a more robust and consistent decision-making approach regardless of the challenge or situation we are presented with.

Process, Consistency, and Resilience

As already mentioned, achieving peak performance requires a dedicated focus to the vision or mission. However, peak performance cannot be achieved without first adopting the same dedication and attitude to the daily processes, which are the building blocks of peak performance. Peak performance is commonly measured through external outcomes. Although it is important to measure performance outcomes that align with the end goal or vision, it can also distract from the steps needed to achieve that end goal.

The daily processes and the habits we cultivate are what allow peak performance to be achieved. As suggested by Darren Hardy in the book *The Compound Effect*, small incremental improvements consistently achieved over time can create exponential growth. This principle of consistency and the compound effect can be applied in a multitude of settings. For example, in the pursuit of peak performance supported by strength and power development for elite athletes, the idea of training consistency is a cornerstone in achieving this. One training session alone will not allow an athlete to achieve peak performance, no matter how hard they work. However, a clear and focused plan executed consistently over days, weeks, months, and even years is the only way to achieve peak performance.

It is important to remember that on the road to achieving success or peak performance, even the best plans coupled with a methodical dedication will encounter obstacles and setbacks. The ability to be resilient and maintain focus, with an unrelenting dedication to the plan or process directed towards the goal or vision, will be a key differentiator between achieving mediocrity or peak performance. Adopting a growth mindset and having the ability to "fail forward," as coined by John C. Maxwell, will allow us to keep improving during the challenging periods of our endeavours. This concept can be applied in almost any situation; for example, a key training principle that underpins any good strength and power programme utilises the principle of progressive overload. This overload can be achieved through various strategies, via increasing intensity, volume, or complexity of work executed. This overload creates a new challenge for the body and pushes it out of homeostasis or equilibrium, which drives the body to adapt to meet the novel stress or demand. If this cycle is repeated at the appropriate rate consistently over time, we see improvements in performance and higher levels of resilience against the previous stressor.

Objective Targets and Thresholds

The use of monitoring key performance indicators (KPIs) relative to established targets or thresholds can be an effective method to help achieve peak performance. The use of monitoring metrics is highly prevalent in many businesses and sporting organisations. Monitoring metrics can be extremely effective in many situations, such as the development of strength and power in elite athletes. Monitoring established KPIs can provide feedback to the athlete themselves and provide context on how they are performing relative to the established targets and thresholds. Monitoring KPIs also allows the performance coach to assess how the athletes are responding and whether those responses are in line with what they would expect, based on the intervention or course of action taken. Finally, it provides accountability with regards to changes in performance relative to the established KPIs, which ultimately aligns with the overall goal or vision.

The use of objective targets and thresholds can also help provide individuals with an understanding of their strengths and weaknesses, thus providing direction for areas of growth or focus. The use of targets helps provide a goal to work towards, which will improve performance related to the overall goal. This helps individuals and teams also understand what their strengths or x-factor qualities are, which can allow them to lean into their strengths to differentiate themselves from other competitors. This is never more evident in elite sport than when individuals or teams devise a game plan to optimise their strengths against their opponents. For example, a team may have put a big emphasis on strength and power development to physically dominate teams and base their game plan around that strength. This principle can also be applied in a business setting; for example, establishing that the customer service component of the business outperforms the rest of the market and can be leveraged to drive more business through positive customer reviews and customer referrals. It is important to have a clear understanding of what differentiates us from the crowd.

Although understanding our strengths is key to achieving peak performance, it is also important to understand and establish minimum thresholds to help avoid weakness or elements that may take away from peak performance. Again, using the elite sport analogy, the team that bases their game plan around utilising their strength and power to their advantage also needs to be mindful of their skill level and their ability to know and learn the tactics to execute the game plan. If this is neglected and it becomes a weakness, it will take away from their overall performance and the team will be unable to utilise their strengths effectively. Once again this is the same in business; we cannot solely focus on what we are good at. We need to keep a balanced view of our strengths and weaknesses using targets and thresholds relative to the overall performance goal to ensure we are turning our strengths into x-factor qualities. At the same time, we need to improve our weaknesses, so they do not limit our performance.

Ultimately the use of these targets and thresholds should be used to help us keep focused on things that align with our overall goal or vision, while helping individuals and teams within organisations continue to improve through reflective practice. The method of utilising targets and thresholds should not be used to direct and pressure employees to hit targets or deadlines without a deeper meaning than just hitting targets. This does not promote autonomy and connection to the overall vision or mission. When this method is used positively and consistently over time, it cultivates a personal responsibility or accountability towards the vision and can play an important role in achieving peak performance.

People and Culture

This section was not left until last because it is the least important. It is the final section as it is arguably the most important, and it is important to have these ideas fresh in our mind when piecing all the concepts together. A sometimes neglected or forgotten element of achieving peak performance within any team or organisation is the consideration of the people themselves. Although it is important to have measurable outcomes to track and drive performance, these outcome measures should not be the foundations on which a team is built. As demonstrated by many great leaders or organisations, by getting the right people on board and giving them a purpose, they can develop a personal connection to that purpose or vision, which will lead to high-performance over time, in a much greater and sustainable way. Only if people feel valued and they are contributing to something bigger than themselves, can a deep connection and investment be cultivated towards the vision and peak performance achieved. A good example in the context of elite sport, and more specifically within the context of athletic development, is if an athlete feels the coach genuinely cares for them, both on a professional and personal level, they are much more likely to trust the coach's decisions. One way to achieve this in a sporting context is through clarity and transparency with regards to the training principles and philosophies being used, and most importantly how they relate to improving the athlete's performance in their given sport. The coach should couple this with developing a relationship and a connection with the athlete on a personal level, so they feel the coach knows and cares about them as a person, which also allows for more effective coaching through a better understanding of that athlete.

As stated by Theodore Roosevelt, "People don't care how much you know, until they know who much you care." This concept is not only important at the micro-level in terms of personal interactions, but to develop a culture that can attain peak performance, this philosophy of caring for each other is crucial for growth across the whole team or organisation as this helps develop trust and a "team spirit." Also, when individuals and team members feel safe amongst their peers and co-workers, it breeds the opportunity to challenge each other through robust conversations. In a non-threatening environment these challenging or robust interactions can be viewed as integral for allowing the team to grow and for creating opportunities for individuals to adopt a growth mindset, which is crucial for improvement.

Conclusion

When we come back to the concept of peak performance and how we can achieve it, both for ourselves and the teams we work with, we must hold ourselves accountable to the principles and values we set for ourselves, along with the principles and values that align with the vision or mission of the organisation we work with. To achieve peak performance in any setting, be it business or sport, we must adopt a tireless approach towards living those values daily. This should be supported by building and utilising our processes, which consistently align with our vision and values.

About the Author

Jonathan Harris-Wright is an experienced athletic performance coach who has spent over a decade assisting amateur, academy, and elite athletes achieve peak performance in their given sport, specialising in strength and power development. This spans a vast array of experiences from developing and growing long-term athletic pathways, to optimising elite athletes for international competitions and managing multidisciplinary teams across various sporting organisations. More recently Jonathan has been managing the performance and science department within a start-up in the smart wearables market.

Jonathan's experience base in achieving peak performance with individuals and teams has been supported through formal education in the areas of optimising physical performance, as well as high-impact leadership and management. The combination of extensive personal experience in multiple high-performance environments supported with formal education around performance and leadership, has allowed Jonathan to develop a deep appreciation and understanding of what it takes to achieve peak performance.

Email: jh-wright@hotmail.com
Twitter: @jonnyhw12

CHAPTER ELEVEN
MENTAL IMAGERY: A SKILL FOR ATHLETES

by Matt Helke
Peak Performance & Baseball Coach, Author, Mentor
Troy, Ohio

What is now proved was once only imagined.
—William Blake

There are a lot of things in sports that athletes can't control. Things such as the weather, their opponents, officials, and fans, just to name a few. But when the dust clears, there are two things that athletes can control: their physical body and their mind. Unfortunately, when it comes to training these two controllable facets of athletic performance, most athletes, coaches, and parents spend their precious time working only on the physical aspect of performing. They basically ignore all the research showing the brain's power to make performance significantly better.

We do not perform any physical skill in isolation. The fact is, our body does not function unless directed to do so by the brain first. It literally coordinates everything we think, feel, and do. For athletes, training the brain for better performance is essential. This is called mental skills training.

While there are many different mental skills, the most important for an athlete to develop is called mental imagery or visualization. The concept itself is pretty straightforward to understand—you mentally rehearse how you want to perform in reality. But I want you to think for a moment. When you hear "mental imagery" or "visualization," what comes to mind? The ability to create vivid pictures in your head, perhaps?

Over the past 30 years, I have heard countless times, "I've tried to do mental imagery (aka visualization) and can't. It's just too hard to do." What I have found is when athletes hear "mental imagery" or "visualization," they instantly impose high expectations as to what they *think* should be involved. They believe they need to create ultra-high-definition pictures in their head to be successful. That it has to have a certain level or quality, and they put a pass-fail criterion on it. If that's what you think too, you are misleading yourself.

What Exactly Is Mental Imagery?

When many athletes hear "mental imagery," they automatically think "seeing." Despite the word's connotation, imagery is not focused solely on visual representations or mental images. The truth is, it refers to a full scope of sensory experiences, including internal emotions and physical sensations. This includes kinesthetics (body movements), touch, sounds, words, thoughts, and feelings (emotions). Studies have shown that people who were born without the ability to see can still generate mental images. Aaron James who has been blind since birth explained, "Totally blind people, from birth, have a mental image in their minds. For us, it's just made of smells, tastes, sounds, and tactile memories. It's all what we use to imagine other things too."

Secondly, and what most people don't realize, is that mental imagery is actually a subset of imagination. The word "imagination" comes from the Latin verb *imaginari* meaning "to picture oneself." Simply put, your imagination is what allows you to create mental imagery. But the word "imagination" gets a bad rap because imagination is commonly thought to be the opposite of reality. There is a stigma attached to the word "imagination." Using the imagination is oftentimes reserved for kids and seems like a childish thing to do. But take a moment and look around you. Chances are only a small fraction of what you see is not a product of human imagination. Computers, cars, and airplanes were all imagined first. Imagination is the very thing that has shaped most of what you see in your everyday, real world.

For the rest of the chapter the terms "imagery," "mental imagery," and "imagination" will be synonymous. Why? Because no mental activity is more prominently linked with mental imagery than that of imagining.

Why Imagery Works

Several decades of research demonstrates beyond any doubt that imagery is a powerful tool in all forms of sports, athletics, and physical performance. It produces measurable gains in performance for both cognitive and physical tasks. According to neuroscientist Dr. Sarah McKay, studies using fMRI, which specifically looks at different mental processes and functions of the brain, show imagery works because the neurons in our brain interpret our thoughts as equivalent to real life action. The fMRIs of the brain show that similar brain areas that are activated in an actual movement are also activated during imagery. Science calls this "functional equivalence." Basically, our brain cannot tell the difference between something that is real or what we are imagining. The following are just two studies to illustrate.

Study One—"Mind Over Matter" by Shackell, Erin & Standing, Lionel (2007)

In this study 30 male university athletes, including football, basketball, and rugby players, were randomly assigned into three groups. The first group only performed mental training of their hip flexor muscles. The second group only used weight machines to physically exercise their hip flexors. The third group, or control group, received neither mental nor physical training. The hip strength of each group was measured before and after training.

- The physical strength of the mental practice only group increased by 24%.
- The physical strength of the physical training only group increased by 28%.
- The physical strength of the control group who didn't do physical or mental training did not change.

Study Two—"Mental Practice" by Richardson, Alan (1967)

Three groups of students were chosen at random. None had ever practiced imagery. On day one, all three groups shot free throws to get their baseline. Once the baseline was recorded:

- Group 1 practiced free throws for one hour a day, every day for 20 days. They did no imagery.

- Group 2 spent 20 minutes every day only mentally shooting free throws. If they "missed," they "practiced," getting the next shot right. Not only were they instructed to "see" the ball go through the hoop, but they were also to imagine and incorporate as many other senses as they could—to "feel" the ball in their hands and its weight and texture; to "hear" the ball swoosh through the net and then bounce on the court.
- Group 3 did not practice at all after the first day.

On the twentieth day they measured the percentage of improvement in each group.

- Group 1 that practiced shooting free throws improved 24%.
- Group 2 that only mentally imagined shooting free throws improved 23%
- Group 3 that did not practice at all after the first day did not improve at all.

What If I'm "Not Good" at Creating Mental Images?

It's true, some people can create good images in their head while others seem to have difficulty. I have to confess; I am one of those people who have a hard time seeing or creating really good mental images. But what I have found for myself and others I have worked with is if you describe what you want to "see" or "do," using your inner speech and incorporating other sensory experiences relating to the act you want to perform, it can have a profound positive effect.

Below is a simple example of how to start to work on your mental images. You can do it on your own, but if you are just starting out, it might be helpful to find someone to talk you through the first few times. This is called guided imagery. The example uses an apple, but you can use any object you want. After each suggestion, pause for at least five seconds. Longer if needed. There is no need to respond verbally. Just think about what is asked. Please remember, this is a simple beginning.

The Apple

- Close your eyes, take a couple deep, controlled breaths, and relax.
- Now just think of an apple.

- Is it a big apple or a small apple?
- As you are thinking of the apple, what color is the apple?
- So, as you are thinking of your colored apple, does it have a stem on top or any leaves?
- Where is the apple? Is it hanging on a tree? In a fruit bowl? On a table?
- Now imagine it is to your right. (You might notice your eyes shifting right.)
- Now imagine it is on your left. (You might notice your eyes shifting left.)
- Now imagine it is back to where it was when you first thought about it.
- Open your eyes. Exercise done.

The act of just thinking of the word "apple" creates a mental image even though it is just a word. You might not actually see a vivid picture of an apple in your mind—yet just by the simple act of thinking of the word—you do. A study by a Harvard Medical School research team published in the journal *NeuroImage* confirmed this fact. Research participants reported generating visual images regardless of whether their intent was to mentally visualize something or when they just thought of it verbally (inner speech). Even though the imagery created differed in clarity between participants, they all created mental images. Their research indicates that visual thinking is deeply ingrained in the brain.

First-Person or Third-Person Point of View Imagery

First-person point of view imagery refers to a person mentally experiencing a situation as if they are actually physically doing it themselves. Third-person point of view imagery refers to a person mentally experiencing a situation as if observing themselves from the outside in the situation. I want to address this specifically because there are differing opinions of which is better. I spoke with Jim Davies, PhD professor of cognitive science and the director of the Science Imagination Laboratory at Carleton University, and asked if either first-person or third-person point of view imagery is better than the other. While he states he doesn't know of any scientific data that shows that one is better than the other, he offered the following:

I know when people are asked to imagine in the third person, when they talk about it, they tend to reflect on non-sensory functions. So, if you ask somebody to imagine unlocking a door for example, they say things like "I'm trying to get in" or "I am unlocking." On the other hand, if you ask somebody to imagine unlocking a door in the first person and ask what it is like, they will say things like "I feel the resistance of the lock slightly as I turn the key." They talk about what it feels like. They can see the hand going from the bottom of their visual field toward the lock. When imaging from the third person, it's almost like they step back physically, which also causes a step back in terms of a higher-level view of what they are trying to do rather than the tactical sensory things.

So, from a visual aspect, the first-person point of view is better, right? Not necessarily because it depends on the aim of the visualization. For instance, using visualization to learn a new technique or mechanic or just wanting to improve on it? What is the athlete wanting to accomplish—is it conceptual (form-based task) or specific and detailed (technical skill)? The sport an athlete participates in might also influence which point of view would be better.

Here are two simplistic examples to better illustrate this. The first: say a baseball player wants to mentally imagine learning to hit a curveball. The first thing he would want to do is to learn how to identify an incoming curveball. This is more of a specific technical skill, so it would favor the first-person point of view. From the first-person view, he would imagine standing in the batter's box looking out at the pitcher. He would see the ball out of the pitcher's hand and imagine the velocity and shape of a curveball's flight coming towards him. His perspective takes on the viewpoint that he is actually experiencing the event, which helps in to develop where his body is in space in relation to a moving object and his timing. Both of these are pretty important in most sports. If he were to use the third-person point of view, he wouldn't experience firsthand any perspective of the curveball's velocity or shape.

The second example: now consider a gymnast wanting to improve their backflips. The third-person view would probably work best in this case. Why? First, the athlete has already learned and performed the flip. Secondly, gymnasts "spot" when they rotate. This means they will focus their sight on one spot as long as possible through the rotation. Doing a flip is about height and

MENTAL IMAGERY: A SKILL FOR ATHLETES

a strong tuck position. This is more about form versus a specific technical skill, so this is why it would favor the third-person point of view. From the first-person view, they would only be looking at one spot, not "seeing" themselves getting the right height or tuck position.

But, please note, an athlete's personal preference should also be taken into consideration. The approach that works best for you is the right one.

The Secret for Developing Better Imagery

One of the most highly regarded models for mental imagery is the PETTLEP model of imagery developed by Holmes and Collins (2001). Most athletes who have been trained in mental imagery have probably been trained using this model. I use this model myself when I introduce athletes to mental imagery. It's too long to include in this chapter, but if you're interested in what it entails, go to *Podium Sports Journal* at www.podiumsportsjournal.com/2010/12/20/using-pettlep-imagery-to-enhance-sports-performance/.

This model is very good and has helped countless athletes. But in my 30-plus years of experience working with athletes, I have identified another key component. You see, studies have shown that even though mental imagery can be vivid and detailed images, most people have rather poor memory for the details. Most remember meaning and feeling much more easily than details. Taking that into consideration, I now incorporate the following into my imagery training.

Define How You Would Like to Perform

First, define how you would like to perform in as much detail as you can. Begin by writing down how you would like to perform. Writing the details down first before doing mental imagery will help make your imagery more focused. Detail the description using all your senses and any associated positive emotions before actually doing imagery or following the PETTLEP or any other model. It is important to create or recreate the content of the image as realistically as possible, so feel yourself right into the situation. Take into account things like:

- What you would see and what you would do physically?
- How would it feel both physically and emotionally?
- What you might hear?

- How you might act after successfully accomplishing the thing you are imagining?

You can take it even further and imagine:

- What might teammates or coaches say after you accomplished what you were imagining?
- What would you find yourself doing that would imply that you did what you were imagining?

Remember in the free throw shooting experiment? The researcher noted the imagery only group wasn't only to imagine seeing the ball going through the hoop. The participants also were to incorporate as many of the other senses as they could. To "feel" the ball in their hands, noting its weight and texture. To "hear" the ball swoosh through the net and bounce on the court.

Stop Wanting to Be It

If you want to perform a particular way, then stop wanting to be it. Wanting is defined as "a lack or deficiency of something" and keeps you in a negative mindset. When you are imagining, you must assume you are doing it now, as if it were true in the present, even though your outer world might say differently at the time. You must be persistent in that assumption. Do not allow your perceived reality to infiltrate. You must be persistent in your mental imagining by staying true to your thoughts.

This can be a tough one. Every day we are bombarded with negativity. We are even tough on ourselves. In 2005, the National Science Foundation published an article regarding research about the number of thoughts humans have per day. They found the average person has between 12,000 and 60,000 thoughts per day. Of those, 80 percent are negative and 95 percent are exactly the same repetitive thoughts they had the day before. So not allowing negativity to leak into our mental imagery can take some time to control. But you can start to take control. When you find yourself being pulled into negativity, doubt, or frustration, that's your cue to stop it in its tracks. Say something simple to redirect those unwanted thoughts, something as simple as "That's not part of my belief system anymore."

When to Do Imagery

Imagery can be done just about anytime and anywhere. One of the best times is when you go to bed. Once you are settled in and relaxed, start your imagery. Here you have the time to give your imagery all the life and vigor you want, and you can repeat the imagery over several times without external distractions. Your imagery should be the last thing you remember before you fall off to sleep. I recommend doing it no less than three times per week. The length is up to you, but I suggest doing it for at least 15 minutes or more.

While pre-game imagining will be shorter, it should still be as lifelike as possible and take three to five minutes. One of the benefits of pre-game imagining is that many times you will already be hearing the sounds of the game. You will be in your athletic uniform (physical feel) or psyched up for the game (emotional feel). You might even be smelling the smells associated with your sport. All these will help you in your imagery.

Last-minute imaging is the shortest of all but still can have a profound effect. This imagining will likely take just a few seconds. Even though it is shorter in length and not as detailed, it will still be influential. As an example, I tell my batters as they are settling into the batter's box to quickly look out onto the diamond. Don't look at the players in the field, look where they are not. Imagine the spot where you want the ball to land and how it will feel when it's hit there.

It is hard to articulate what you see in your own mind's eye or even how it compares with everyone else's. The fact is, it differs between individuals, so don't try to live up to someone else's imagery standard. Studies are revealing how our imaginations shape the world we perceive and make us who we are. Imagination helps us to reprogram our way of thinking and, therefore, our way of doing. But as with any learned skill, it can become less accessible if we don't use it consistently.

Bottom line, individuals who can create vivid mental pictures generally have better results than those who can't do it as well. They simply perform better. Even if not done perfectly, you will still see improvement. By adding imagery to your training program, you will become a better and more complete athlete who can reach peak levels of performance. As I tell my athletes, "If you don't imagine things being different than they are, nothing will change."

About the Author

Coach Matt Helke has a BS in psychology with emphasis in perception and cognition from Wright State University. Coach Helke is a performance optimization mentor for all sports and has been an active baseball coach since 1992. His certifications include sports psychology coach (Ed), biomechanics specialist, visual guided imagery specialist, core conditioning specialist, and training in applied neuroscience and brain health. He is also an accredited interscholastic coach. He is founder of The Baseball Observer Digital Magazine, Directory & Training, and 360 Peak Performance. He is a member of the NFHS, ABCA, OHSBCA, and ISBS (International Society of Biomechanics in Sports), and is a professional affiliate of APA Div. 47 (Society for Sport, Exercise and Performance Psychology). Coach Helke has worked with numerous players, coaches, and teams at all levels.

Email: coachhelke@360peakperformance.com
Website: http://www.thebaseballobserver.com
"You're not a clone, so why train like one?"

CHAPTER TWELVE
SEEK TO UNDERSTAND BEFORE YOU SEEK TO BE UNDERSTOOD

By Bashir A. Ismail
Performance Coach, FRM Chinese Olympic Committee
Stavanger, Norway

It was another week of preparations. The heat was picking up, even in the early morning hours here in Southern China. I learned the term "dog days" from a website article, as it would get so hot that the outside workers would get an additional relief period during the day. As I commuted to work, I noticed quite a few building projects going on in my neighborhood as well as the long-awaited upgrade to our current sports complex, so I felt a bit sorry for all the people who had to endure this current climate.

My assistants and I prepared the gym floor with mats, foam rollers, bands, and small massage balls as part of our athletes' pre-workout routine. We would also, on the first training day of the week, set up equipment, such as force plates and handgrip dynamometers, as part of our weekly training readiness and progress assessment.

The diving athletes arrived at the gym on separate e-bikes. Wei arrived first. She had a jovial spirit and always greeted me with a warm smile before she changed to her training gear. Her diving partner, Hui, arrived a few minutes later. She was the quieter one of the two. She normally greeted me with eye contact and a smile as well. On this day, she arrived with what I interpreted as a slightly sad face. I took note and allowed the girls to settle in and prepare for the strength session we had planned.

With the mats and self-massage tools on the floor, I always like to give my athletes at least four to five minutes to self-massage their bodies to loosen up prior to the warm-up. Sometimes, this helps alleviate the perception of soreness or morning stiffness, which is very helpful before transitioning to the warm-up. I also like to use this initial period to catch up with what they did over the weekend and at the same time gauge their mood and recovery from the past week's technical training and strength session. They normally train on weekends, but this past weekend, the technical coach made them do something different. They performed an explosive jump-training session at the nearby track. It involved consecutive forward jumps, which they named "frog jumps." They were very familiar with the exercise and had done it multiple times throughout their career, but it had been a while since the last time. As a result, they reported to me as well as on the training questionnaire that they were sore in the legs afterwards.

Wei stated she was sore but thought she could handle today's strength and power session. I could sense in her voice and spirit that she could deal with today's training demand. I was not surprised. I didn't recall a single time in the past year we'd worked together that she was in a poor mood or too fatigued to perform our planned sessions. Her partner seemed to be more affected by this past weekend's jump training. She reported that she slept poorly as well. This was reasonable, but I still had a sense that there was something else going on with her.

We were a small group of people in the gym: my assistants, me, and the two athletes. Prior to the warm-up, Hui kindly asked me if she could do less work during our session. I responded that I would think about it. From my experience, I know that mood and energy levels can change once we engage in activity, so I left the decision to be made till after the warm-up. After the initial period of self-massage, we normally perform our weekly performance assessment, which includes a handgrip strength assessment and different types of jumps measured on a force-plate. Briefly, I use these measures to objectively evaluate the athlete's training progress and current readiness to train. After we performed the hand grip test, I decided to forego the jump assessments. I noticed from the body language and movement of the two divers that they were still sore, so there was no point in performing this assessment.

After the general warm-up, we continued with specific preparation that I and my assistants led. Hui's mood was now slightly better as I tried to tease a smile out of her. The theme of the session was lower-body strength and power, along with injury prevention work. Our gym was relatively small, and we were not the only group working there, so we had the girls do different exercises and rotated accordingly. This allowed me to be with one athlete at one time and my assistants would support the other.

Hui repeated her request about cutting the workout short. I replied that if she gave me high-quality execution on the main exercises, I would reduce the training volume on the subsequent movements. She somewhat agreed and carried on. Hui was performing the first exercise with good form and intent, but she seemed to lose her concentration and presence after the first few repetitions. When this continued into the second set, I went up to her during her rest period and asked if something was bothering her. She shook her head and said, "I am fine," in her English, but the interpreter and I knew something was different. I decided to not go any further with this, and we continued our session with reduced workload.

When we completed our sessions, we would always finish up with a cooldown stretch and talk some more with the divers about how the session went and other general stuff. Wei seemed to have gotten back her energy and was pretty talkative by the end of the session. That was Wei's jolly, go-lucky spirit. The lightened training workload seemed to have done the trick. On the other hand, Hui didn't say much, and she only spent a brief time stretching before she went to change out of her training gear and leave the gym. I saw this as a moment to chat with her, so the interpreter and I went after her, leaving Wei with my assistants.

We caught up with Hui as she was getting on her e-bike. I approached her more carefully about what was bothering her. When I mentioned that she was very different from our previous sessions, she opened up. She revealed that the last few weeks had been rough mentally, and now she'd begun to feel it physically as well. It all began during the COVID-19 pandemic, with significant restrictions, including loss of training opportunities and competition participation. Earlier in the year, she and Wei hadn't qualified for the Tokyo Olympics, even though they'd come in second in the national qualifying event. She was very competitive and took these setbacks hard.

Another quadrennial event, the Chinese National Games, was being held just weeks after the Tokyo Olympics. For many Chinese sports and disciplines, this competition is ranked above the Summer Olympics. The competitive level is comparatively greater in many disciplines, diving being one of them. Therefore, it was common to see technical coaches significantly increase the technical training volume during the late spring and summer months.

Hui's mood response reflected all this. Hui admitted that she was not even sure if she would make it to the national games. When I asked her why, she revealed that she was planning on retiring this season. This took me by surprise as she was still young, healthy, and competitive. But after I reviewed what she disclosed about the previous year's events, I got a sense of the immense demand placed on her, from her coaches, our sports organization, and even her own expectations. Slowly the picture became clearer to me, what was going through her mind that affected her performance in our session. I apologized to her for not having understood this at an earlier point. She smiled and was grateful to me for seeking her out and for my willingness to listen to her request to modify her workout.

I always thought I knew how my athletes felt and what was on their mind by observing their behavior. This experience with Hui taught me that I had to peel the onion another layer. Now, when I notice an athlete behaving in ways I am not used to seeing, instead of assuming it is just related to their physical state, fatigue and so on, I realize it might well be a composite of other factors that could be out of their control. This is when it becomes critical for me to seek to understand before I seek to be understood.

The sport of diving has a long tradition and became part of the Summer Olympic Games early last century. It resembles similar acrobatic features as observed in gymnastics and, as such, requires a great degree of body-awareness and coordination. In individual and synchronized diving, the athletes are evaluated and scored throughout the different phases of the performance as soon as they begin to move on the platform or springboard. Each attempt commences with the approach, then the hurdle, the preparation jump, the take-off jump, and the characteristic flight phase where we all recognize the difficult maneuvers being performed before it all ends with the water entry. A successful high-degree-of-difficulty dive is often scored highly when the water splash is kept to a minimum. This makes the sport of diving highly complex and very challenging from a psychological and physical perspective.

China has emerged as a powerhouse in all diving events in the past 30 years. This is not a coincidence as the preparation for competing in the sport begins at a very early age. Once an athlete is selected for the sport, it is not uncommon to see participation age as low as 6 to 8 years old. Early specialization is, therefore, not uncommon to see in sports such as gymnastics and diving, as our bodies and, in particular, the brain, are at an ideal phase of life where all forms of learning are very adaptable. As such, athletes devote large amounts of training in such sports. It is common for young athletes to train five to seven hours daily, six days a week on diving-related training. Considering the coaching demand and training quality, among other things, it is not uncommon to see relatively young divers become successful on the world stage even before the age of 15. With China's successful history in the sport, diving has become even more competitive domestically. It's not uncommon to read about world champions and Olympic medalists losing out to fellow countrymen and women in the Chinese National Games, the world's largest sporting event. As such, the pressure to succeed is very high for the coach and Chinese athlete.

As we were approaching the final weeks before the Chinese National Games, or the "Big Dance," as I coined it to my athletes, the technical training naturally became the emphasis of our preparation. Our physical preparation sessions were now down to once per week. I could see a noticeable change in Hui's mood and energy. I also made sure to visit diving training sessions and could observe the deep concentration Hui displayed when preparing and performing dives. She was now smiling and goofing around more between dives, seemingly displaying she now was feeling better and coping with the increasing competition pressure. Her efforts in the gym became more consistent, and we had an open dialogue about what she could do with good effort and execution to optimize her performance. Hui was still determined that this was very likely her very last competition, but I could sense that she wanted to end her career on a good note. With this in mind, I tried to motivate her with the satisfaction of finalizing her career with a medal finish, in a similar way as when she'd entered the world stage and had taken a gold medal.

Both of our divers were very excited for the upcoming event as there had been so many disruptions and uncertainties related to if the event would be held at all. When the diving competition commenced, our staff was watching the events on the big screens in our gym. I felt a mix of excitement and nervousness when we finally got the chance to watch Wei and Hui compete. In the synchronized event, they met stiff competition and were, for a long period, chasing a podium finish. Small errors could result in significant impact on point scoring given by the seven judges evaluating the diving athletes. Our diving athletes ended with a respectable eighth place in this event, but I noticed in their body language that they had been hopeful of a better placement.

On the following day, it was the individual event in the 3-meter spring-board dive. This was Hui's main event aside from the synchronized competition. I was feeling the same level of excitement and nervousness all over again. She was now in control of her performance to a greater extent. When she appeared on the screen, her concentration was unmistakable from what I'd seen during her last couple of sessions back home. The competition entailed five diving attempts, and among the competitors was the recent Olympic champion. All competitors normally begin the competition with a dive of lower difficulty. This was likely helpful to ease the nerves and build confidence for the following attempts.

Hui steadily increased the difficulty of her dives, and she was remarkably stable. For the trained eye, this meant how she controlled her extremities when transitioning between different patterns of movement while in flight and the following water entry. Most viewers largely judge the performance based on how much "splash" the divers make. After observing quite a few training dives back at our facility, I could sometimes discern an average performance from a great one, validated by the technical coach when I listened to their feedback.

Hui maintained her consistency in performance and displayed smooth yet accurate performance with very low point deduction. It became a nail-biter down to the final two attempts. In the standings, she was just behind her former national team-member mate and recent Olympic gold medalist. The competitor chasing Hui received point deduction, and Hui was only one successful dive away from securing her spot. She still had a chance to pass the Olympic champion on the then second place who was going for another gold finish but who was chasing the leader who was the event's major surprise.

The final two to three dives are the ones that often separate contenders. Hui produced her best and most consistent performance at the whole competition during the final attempts. It was now all up to her and likely the last competitive event in her career. She nailed her final dive, sufficient to cement her podium finish at third place just behind the reigning Olympic gold medalist. I was so happy on her behalf and proud of her overall performance, recalling everything she'd had to endure the last 18 months.

When it was time for the medal ceremony, I saw a different girl. This one was relieved, with a lightened body posture and a bright smile. This moment of relief was what we'd worked for. To live up to our potential during circumstances we cannot always control. I truly believe that the moment we put our athletes in the center of attention and attempt to understand that they are more than just athletes, is where we can achieve greater mutual respect, collaboration, and subsequent improved chances of successful outcomes. This mindset makes the whole process even more rewarding when we experience both the person and athlete succeed.

About the Author

Bashir A. Ismail recently worked in China as a performance coach for the Chinese Olympic Committee and for provincial level sports government, responsible for physical preparation of key athletes for the 2022 Beijing Winter Olympics and the 2021 Chinese National Games. He received his master's degree in strength and conditioning from Springfield College in Massachusetts and his bachelor's degree in sports science from Norwegian School of Sports Sciences. He has accrued over 12 years of experience, coaching youth, recreational to professional athletes, as well as running his own coaching business. Before entering the strength and conditioning profession, Bashir worked in the Norwegian military for nearly five years and subsequently completed a bachelor's degree in optometry and visual science, working as an optometrist until he fully committed to the performance coaching.

Email: b.a.ismail.no@gmail.com
LinkedIn: https://www.linkedin.com/in/bashir-ali-ismail-ms-bsc-optom-cscs-d-rscc-70048345/

CHAPTER THIRTEEN
NUTRITION FOR PEAK PERFORMANCE IN ATHLETES

By Jennifer Kavanagh
Sports Nutritionist, Holistic Health Coach
Myrtle Beach, South Carolina

It is health that is real wealth and not pieces of gold and silver.
—Mahatma Gandhi

Nutrition can be a confusing and overwhelming science to understand. It can also be very contradictory and difficult to sort out. I will try to provide for you the best recommendations on food and nutrition that will help you reach your wellness and performance goals as an athlete. Let's begin with an area many struggle with: how to fuel around your workouts.

Fuel your body properly for the level of activity you do each day. This is critical for peak performance. Many people believe they should exercise in a fasted state to burn more fat. This will never result in top-level athletic performance. Your body needs energy to perform, whether you are hitting the gym to lift weights, doing some high intensity interval training, or training for a marathon or whatever your exercise of choice is. Many women especially try to cut calories drastically and still exercise intensely to try to lose body fat. This is not the way to go. After 15 years as a personal trainer and working with thousands of clients, here is what I find works well.

Early-Morning Workouts

If you work out early in the morning, 30 to 45 minutes prior to your workout, eat a small meal containing a mix of carbs and protein. Some examples might include a piece of whole grain toast with almond butter or a hard-boiled egg with half of a banana. Your body turns to carbohydrates first for energy. I assure you, if you have some carbs in your system, you will be able to lift heavier, run faster, feel better, and recover more efficiently post-workout.

Afternoon or Evening Workouts

If you work out later in the morning, afternoon, or evening you have time for a full meal. You should eat a complete meal two to three hours prior to your workout. You want to make sure you have plenty of carbs for energy along with some protein for fullness and healthy fats. The ratio I like to strive for is about 40/35/25. That is 40 percent of calories coming from healthy whole-food carbohydrates, 35 percent coming from protein, and 25 percent coming from fat. I love a good bowl of oatmeal in the morning. I add a scoop of protein powder and sometimes fruit and nuts. If it's later in the day, you could do soup and a sandwich with a small salad. While I am a huge advocate of eating tons of veggies, they aren't always the best plan prior to a workout.

Post-Workout Nutrition

Many clients tell me they are too busy rushing to work after a workout to eat, allowing several hours to go by before refueling. By then, you are starving and feeling tired and weak because you haven't replenished your body's need for nutrients to rebuild the muscle that you've torn down during your workout. You have a limited window of 30 to 60 minutes where your body is ready for a refuel. You want an easily digestible meal of about half carbs and half protein. I recommend using whey protein as it is easy for your muscles to absorb and has the right combination of amino acids to begin the rebuilding process. A shake is the quickest and easiest to digest post workout. I would suggest adding half a banana or a cup of berries to your shake for carbs. You can also add anything else you like. Nut butter, flax or chia seeds, and almond milk are all good choices and will help keep you full. Then you will need a real meal about one to two hours later again with a good mix of macronutrients: 40 to 45 percent carbs, 30 to 35 percent protein, and about 25 percent fat.

The 80/20 Rule—Eat Whole Foods

Make all your calories count. Make mindful choices 80 to 90 percent of the time. Prepping and planning ahead is the best way to ensure you are getting proper nutrition. Have the right foods in your fridge and have easy things to grab when you are in a hurry. Protein is key here! If you have a health goal such as fat loss, muscle building, speed or agility improvement, or cardio endurance, and you're serious about reaching it, it will take work. You will need to figure out the right number of calories you need to support your training program and break that down into proper macronutrient ratios. A nutritionist specializing in athletes can help you with this.

Do not be overly restrictive! Even if fat loss is your goal, operating on too few calories leads to low energy, poor performance in workouts, and slower recovery. You need fuel. If you are someone who is constantly restricting carbohydrates or calories, it may be time to begin a reverse diet. You will want to gradually increase your calories, giving your body not only the energy it needs to make progress toward your goal, but the micronutrients, vitamins, and minerals that will continue to lead to a healthy lifestyle with less disease, more energy, and no feelings of deprivation, which can often lead to disordered eating patterns like binging. You need calories to rev up that metabolism, or it will actually slow down, which will make any goals of weight loss or muscle gain slow to come or impossible to achieve.

Eat whole foods! Try not to consume "frankenfoods" that you find in many cans and boxes in the interior of the grocery store. These highly processed foods may make for a quick grab but can be highly inflammatory and lead to long-term diseases as well as hinder your progress. Your body doesn't know how to process the chemicals, so it stores them as fat. Think again about that 80/20 rule I keep coming back to: 80 percent of your calories should come from vegetables, fruit, whole grains (rice, oats, quinoa), and lean proteins (fish, seafood, chicken, and occasional pork or beef). That allows 10 to 20 percent of your calories to come from either some sort of processed food, a treat, takeout, or even wine! The bottom line is the better quality food you eat in the right quantities, the better results you will get.

Once you know what you should be eating, you have two primary goals. The first is going to be to hit your protein goal, which is usually a bit higher for athletes than those that don't exercise. The second goal is to keep your calories in the correct range. I say "range" because this is not an exact science, but you need to make sure you are getting enough calories for your body to perform and recover, so you can reach your goal, yet not too many so that you may gain weight or feel sluggish or slow. This will be very different based upon your goals. If you are trying to build muscle, you will need way more calories than someone who is trying to lose body fat.

Macros

Protein is KING! Sometimes it's difficult to reach a high-protein goal. An avid exerciser may need up to one gram of protein per pound of bodyweight. Not everyone will need this much, so it is important to take into account your personal goals, current body weight, age, and gender. Typically, a good range for most athletes is 0.8 to one gram of protein per pound of body weight. Always think about how you can get protein in each meal or snack. Some suggestions to bump up protein would be to find a quality protein shake to have every day, and even some protein bars can help add 20 grams of protein to your day. If you eat animal products, it is much easier. Eggs, chicken, fish or any lean protein adds up quickly, with each four- to six-ounce serving usually having as much as 25 to 30 grams of protein. If you are vegan or vegetarian, you can still get enough protein, but you have to work a little harder using sources like beans, lentils, tofu, tempeh, and vegan protein shakes and bars. It's difficult but doable.

Carbohydrates are just as important for any athlete. Carbohydrates are your body's first go-to source for energy. You need carbs to fuel your workout, to recover, and to give you energy throughout the day. For many years I believed I had to restrict my carbohydrate intake to very low amounts to get the fat loss results I needed. First of all, that became the single biggest reason I became a chronic binge eater. Severe restrictions will always lead to a binge in the end. Also, carbs make us happy. Let's be real. They are comforting, and they taste great. Eat your carbs. The healthier your carbohydrate choices are, the better results you will have, but you can basically have anything in moderation.

That being said, do not be of the mindset that you worked out today so you can eat cake, the entire bread basket, and multiple cocktails that evening. Don't eat your way out of your workout. Again, the 80/20 rule can be applied here as well. Eighty percent of your carbohydrates should be sourced from healthy whole foods like starchy vegetables, whole grains, and fruit! Yes! You can have some sugar, wine, chocolate, chips, whatever you want, but consider them a treat and only 10 percent of your daily calories.

Fat! We all need a small amount of fat to help add flavor to food, keep us full, and absorb vitamins. But many fats have no nutritional value at all and should be reduced or avoided. I recommend eliminating all oils, most butter and saturated fats from cheese (part of your 10 percent), as well as processed meats like bacon and hot dogs. There is no benefit at all to eating any of these fats. Most of your fats should come from healthy sources like salmon, avocado, nuts or nut butters, flax and chia seeds, and lean proteins.

Have a Plan and Learn to Meal Prep

Having a plan is absolutely critical. I suggest choosing one day to plan your meals for the week. Actually schedule this time into your week, so you know it will get done. It doesn't have to be a ton of time. Most people can get away with prepping and cooking twice a week for the entire week. You don't have to cook every day. If you prepare food at home, then you do not end up repeatedly going through a drive-through or ordering takeout because you didn't plan for the day. If you plan, shop, and cook in one day, you can get more than half of your week taken care of. I choose three days a week to cook. I recommend making large batches of foods so you can portion them out into smaller containers that are ready for you to just grab from the fridge and take to work or eat when you are ready. Things like oats, rice, beans, and many veggies can be washed, cut, cooked, or roasted, and are ready to be eaten as a side, a whole meal, or added to recipes throughout the week. Soups, chili, and stews are great to prepare and portion out as well and will last several days in the fridge. Pre-cut, wash, and chop most veggies when you bring them home from the store. Roast large sheet trays of different veggies to have them on hand and ready to use in a recipe or just to eat as a side. All this will save you time later and help to keep you on track throughout the week.

Accountability and Logging Food and Calorie Output

Being accountable is extremely important for anyone trying to achieve an athletic or health goal. If you have a coach, friend, or family member who is willing to help you stay accountable, that is fantastic. However, there are some very useful tools you can use that will help you stay on track.

I highly recommend tracking and logging every bite you put in your mouth. Use an app like My Fitness Pal. If you've never done this, it could be a real eye-opener for you. This will tell you (within a margin of error) how many calories you are consuming and how many grams of each macronutrient you are eating every day. You may be shocked how small things—like eating the crust from your kid's sandwich, tasting while you cook, finishing bites from others' plates, having just one spoonful of ice cream or one piece of chocolate—can add up to hundreds of calories!

The other side of the equation can also be easily tracked. Use a tool like a Fitbit or Apple watch to count your calorie output. These devices are close to accurate. There will always be some degree of error, but you can get a great idea of the range of calories you burn on exercise days versus non-exercise days and the impact of moving more on your calorie expenditure. These two numbers ultimately will determine your outcome.

In summary, nutrition can be tricky. To be at your peak in life, work, fitness, and health you need to follow the 80/20 rule, eat mostly whole foods, figure out and stick to your calorie and macro goals, and most of all be consistent! Just as mindset is important for your workout routines and athletic preparation, a mindset surrounding your nutrition is important. In order to perform at your absolute peak level, the fuel you provide to your body just might be that one component that takes you there.

About the Author

Jennifer Kavanagh has been in the health and fitness business for over 15 years. After successfully losing 70 pounds, she decided to leave the corporate world and focus on helping others get healthy. She began the journey as a certified personal trainer and has continued in the fitness industry now coaching and training hundreds of clients as an Orangetheory Fitness Coach. After a few years in fitness, Jennifer got her certification as a holistic health coach and incorporated her love of fitness into her new weight loss and health business, Living Well Nutrition. Currently while still coaching at Orangetheory, she is helping hundreds of clients get healthy through whole food diet and lifestyle coaching. She supports clients to improve their long-term health, increase their levels of energy, heal inflammation and joint pain, and learn to lose all the weight they desire without crazy restrictions and fad diets. By educating clients about a lifestyle way of eating through long-term sustainable behavior changes with a structured one-on-one customized health plan, Jennifer is helping hundreds lose weight, feel great, break food addictions, and live a healthy life without the chronic cycle of yo-yo dieting and restrictions.

Email: jenniferkkavanagh@gmail.com
Website: www.eatplantsloseweight.com

CHAPTER FOURTEEN
IDENTITY, FREEDOM, AND THE LOVE OF SPORT

By Kristin Kaye
Athlete Coordinator, US Olympic & Paralympic Committee
Lake Placid, New York

"It's impossible," said pride. "It's risky," said experience. "It's pointless," said reason. "Give it a try," whispered the heart.
—Unknown

When I look back on my life, it is difficult not to observe that there has been a clear story unfolding that involves passion for sport, desire for excellence, and joy in sharing my journey with others. From a four-year-old who knew she wanted to continue practicing for another year before participating in her first ice skating show; to the 12-year-old who made her own decision that she would pursue rhythmic gymnastics and devote her youth to training at the highest level; to the 18-year-old who made the choice to fully recover from an eating disorder and return to gymnastics to demonstrate that the sport could be done in a healthy way; to the 24-year-old who knew she wanted to inspire others with her comeback story while attempting another sport (rowing) at the elite level; to the 31-year-old who accepted that it was time to take on a supporting role for other athletes as they pursue their dreams—the topic of sport performance has been with me my entire life.

There is one idea that I believe is the reason I was able to approach what I consider my level of peak performance—once an individual begins to understand that they are not solely defined by their sport, there is a greater sense of freedom to invest in their sport at the highest level, and ultimately reach their greatest performance potential, because the driving force is rooted in a love for the sport rather than in their self-worth being tied to performance and results. A person's greatest potential cannot truly be reached when motivated by pressures from others. Rather, dedication must come from within, and the ultimate motivation must be a genuine enjoyment of the process, however challenging it may be.

I sought advice from those closest to me; however, it was my own decision to pursue gymnastics at the level I did. It was my own decision to make a change, recover from my eating disorder, and never look back; and in rowing, though I had my share of setbacks and ultimately did not accomplish my highest goal, I made the decision to pursue excellence in a completely different sport than gymnastics, and it helped lead me to my current position. Over time I have learned that I am not defined by any one of these decisions, but the reason I was able to tap into a level of peak performance within each of these areas has largely been due to the freedom I experience in doing what I love. Where did that freedom come from? Here are three main strategies and three supplemental tips for developing a mindset for peak performance.

Strategy #1: Know Yourself Apart from Sport

The most impactful strategy I can share for developing a mindset for peak performance is to know yourself apart from sport. One of the greatest lessons eating disorder treatment taught me was the self-acceptance that can come from investing time in exploring one's true identity. During some of my most substantial developmental years as a teenager, I went from not knowing myself apart from identifying as "the gymnast," to not knowing myself apart from identifying with "my eating disorder," to developing such a solid foundation of who I am in my own faith-based values that the freedom of self-acceptance has been a daily way of living for me since my full recovery 15 years ago.

Because of societal pressures, it's not uncommon for individuals to struggle with establishing their identity, and finding it in sport is common, even if unintentional, especially at a young age. I started rhythmic gymnastics when I was eight, and my life revolved around it. I practiced six days a week, left school early for training, and competed often. There was no pressure from my parents or coaches to succeed. I truly just loved the sport so much that knowing myself apart from gymnastics was not even on my radar. At the same time, though, I had begun to develop fears about growing up, misunderstood my perfectionist tendencies, and became preoccupied with thoughts of food.

I believe this identity battle contributed greatly to my struggles with an eating disorder. During my freshman year of high school, it may have appeared to others that I had everything going for me. What more could someone want as a 14-year-old junior national champion? The answer: to love herself just the way she was. How could I not like myself when such amazing opportunities were unfolding? The answer: anorexia nervosa, a severe, self-destructive illness that was thrust into my life, leaving me feeling depressed, isolated, weak, unable to compete like I once had, and dissatisfied with every detail about myself.

When I entered treatment, I was forced to stop gymnastics. The only identity I knew was taken away from me, and the only thing I could do was find a new identity. I realized an identity in the eating disorder had developed. Anorexia had taken control of my life. Eating disorders are very much an outward expression of inward struggles.

It was during a time of personal discovery in a therapy session where my life motives began to change. This is where my current identity began to take shape. That is, an identity in faith-based values, when my therapist suggested I try going to church. I started learning about God's unconditional love and how He has a specific plan for my life, and slowly I started to believe that I was uniquely designed with a greater purpose than I could see. Living with this in mind creates the freedom to not need to have all the answers and be perfect all the time.

There is power in freedom, and when it comes from a higher source, it can ignite a passion for seeking your purpose—and in the case of my sports career, reaching peak performance. I had found my missing piece, and solidifying my identity changed my life's projection from self-destruction to freedom in pursuing my dreams. Joy came from sorrow, and I began to perform from the place I once had, out of pure love for gymnastics rather than striving to be the best at the expense of my health and well-being. It was nearly four years after stopping gymnastics that I felt called to return to the sport, and within six months, I was competing again internationally. Two years later, I became a member of the 2009 US Rhythmic Gymnastics Senior Group Team that competed at the World Championships in Japan.

MINDSET TOOLS FOR ATHLETES

At some point, we all face an identity crossroads of either living up to others' standards or focusing on who we were uniquely created to be. I now have a purpose in caring for my body and living for more than just myself. If God can love and accept me, then I can love and accept myself too, believing that He did not get me wrong. Therapy and treatment programs help in many ways, but the ultimate impact on my recovery was the redemption and transformation I found in a faith-based identity.

Supplemental Tip #1: Know What Personal Qualities You Can Use to Your Advantage

With years of experience as a recovery coach in various eating disorder treatment centers, I have encountered numerous individuals who come from athletic backgrounds, struggling to separate their self-worth from their desire to have a body they consider "perfection." I found myself sharing the message of personal value, worth, and purpose with each client. I hoped people would start discovering the power of their inner qualities rather than listening to the self-deprecation the world so often projects. Intentional self-examination is how I too learned to use many personal qualities to my advantage.

Quite often various qualities that are praised in the athletic world are similar to characteristics seen in those struggling with an eating disorder. Those same qualities can also be used to aid in recovery when we understand how to use these traits in a positive way. Undoubtedly my determination, discipline, and perfectionist tendencies that I used to reach success in gymnastics also helped in my journey of recovery. Ultimately, when I learned that recovery did not mean changing who I was, but rather enhancing who I already am by learning about what my body needs and how to constructively cope with life's challenges, I overcame my eating disorder and returned to a high level of performance.

Self-awareness can aid in better mental preparation and contribute to an individual's ability to respond rather than react to a situation. If something interferes with usual training or competition readiness, the reaction does not need to be an "end-all" mindset to a positive performance, but rather, the potential response can be better managed because the individual is aware of how they handle certain situations, whether that be stress, fear, nervousness, exhaustion, etc., allowing for little to no negative impact on their performance. Understanding how much power your own thoughts hold can set you free to train the way you know you can, or they can send you spiraling downward. In rowing, I could not always tap into the freedom that came with loving the sport enough to train to my greatest potential because I created my own mental roadblocks. My greatest successes came when I pressed pause on my internal negative self-talk and focused solely on executing what I trained every day to do, allowing me to be completely present in the moment.

Strategy #2: Utilize Your Resources

As a young gymnast, I did not necessarily understand what it meant to utilize resources, partly because of a lack thereof. I was fortunate to live near one of the top training facilities and best coaches in the country, and once I reached a level of success, my travel expenses were covered; however, continuous access to certain resources that elite athletes might have in more popular sports or a college athletic department, such as training equipment, traveling physical therapists, massage therapists, sport psychologists, and dietitians, were not always available to me or they were expensive. As an adult rower, I continued learning the challenges of trying to reach an elite level even if access to private coaching or recovery tools were limited due to the demands of living on my own.

Years of training taught me that if you have access to resources, use them because a lack of resources can impact the growth of an athlete. In my current position, I often see that resources are there, but not used. Because athletes are usually so focused on sport performance, the holistic development of themselves is often pushed to the wayside. I regularly observe that the type of resource usually determines usage. Sports medicine services, for example, have immediate impact, but interest in other "life skills" programs is not as enticing because the immediate impact may not be seen. Without taking the focus away from achieving sport excellence, it is possible to enhance yourself both physically and mentally in ways that can positively influence your current athletic goals and also benefit you in the future.

Supplemental Tip #2: Develop an Attitude of Gratitude

Perspective can change the way a person approaches sport and life. When privilege and rights get confused, it can often lead to frustration for what a person does not have rather than gratitude for what they do. Complaining is exhausting, whereas gratitude for where a person is at can be life-giving.

Gratitude can lead an individual to focus on things they can control (e.g., how they choose to show up to practice each day, how they respond to setbacks, criticism, or the word "no"), but an entitled attitude can lead to focusing on things out of their control (e.g., who is supporting or not supporting them, if they are not getting what they feel is deserved). This, in turn, can be draining, leading to a negative impact on their energy and capacity to consistently train at a high level.

One of the opportunities I had as a gymnast was to train at both the Lake Placid and Colorado Springs US Olympic & Paralympic Training Centers. It was an honor and a privilege to train among others also at the top of their sports. It is interesting to be in my current position, once again at the location where I was at my best as a gymnast. The same feelings of honor and privilege ring true to my work today. After my experiences in rowing, however, I quickly realized how much of an advantage it is for athletes to live and train in one location and have many of life's details (like meals) taken care of for them. So much so that at times I wonder if this takes a toll on learning what it is like to live independently beyond the training center walls.

I used to think that asking for help was a sign of weakness; however, I have discovered that asking for help and seeking support when needed does not mean you are inadequate. Making assumptions and jumping to conclusions can inhibit a growth mindset; however, being curious and inquisitive has the potential to propel you forward. When an athlete thinks they are not being supported, there is an added level of stress that comes from playing defense with others, be it coaches, teammates, or family members. Control what you can, and leave the rest be. Approach others with gratitude and ask for help, and positive partnerships can develop that aid in reaching peak performance.

Strategy #3: Strive for Balance and Allow for Change

Being an elite-level gymnast at such a young age, I knew no different than learning to manage training with schoolwork. When I transitioned to rowing, I had to adapt to training around several part-time jobs and then later online graduate school. During a brief college rowing coach position, I observed the impact of quality over quantity training due to restricted training allotments. My current position now allows me to observe many athletes whose primary job is training. In these various scenarios, one recurring theme is balance. Some may say a person's greatest athletic potential can only be reached by giving complete focus to the goal; however, there is a very real place for seeking a balanced life while also striving to attain peak performance. Reaching your peak does require 100 percent focus, but not necessarily all the time. Balance can aid in enhancing your mental focus while training and ultimately lead to your optimal performance.

Physical recovery is essential; however, continuously turning down all non-sport-related activities because of concern for their possible impact on recovery can limit the potential for personal development. Remember that personal development is linked to self-awareness, which can lead to understanding your purpose more fully, and ultimately can have a significant impact on the attainability of peak performance. Having a routine is common for athletes and not a bad thing. Not every change will benefit you; however, give change a chance, whether that be with training or building a balanced life. Your body can learn to adapt to a new normal that actually enhances performance.

Here are two examples: doing full routines in gymnastics obviously takes effort. At a competition you want to be ready to give your best effort when it counts. The summer before I won the junior national championships, I was working with my coach who, during practices, observed that my second routine was consistently better than my first. So, I began to do an entire routine behind the curtain prior to going out onto the competition floor. Contrary to my original concern, I was not more tired—instead, I felt more ready.

It was similar with rowing—I used to think I could not expend a lot of energy during my warm-up because I would use it all up before the race, but when I started trying a longer warm-up, I found it was actually easier to tap into that full-effort feeling during the race. This may not work for everyone, but the point is, not trying something immediately eliminates the potential to learn something that may help you better achieve success.

Supplemental Tip #3: Understand When It Is Appropriate to Adjust Priorities

I missed my fair share of family events and school activities due to training. These are the sacrifices that being at the top of your sport may require, but as explained earlier, sport does not need to be your complete identity. Training periods naturally ebb and flow, and being intentional with mapping out how you will create balance may be necessary. Adjusting priorities allows you the ability to step away from the constant pressures of performing and remember why you do what you do. Hopefully, it is a genuine love for the sport that ignites your passion to pursue excellence in an activity that you have been gifted in and there is a desire to return.

That is why I came back to gymnastics after treatment. That is why I attempted another sport at the elite level. And that is why it was also a natural transition for me to quietly leave my training environment with rowing, earn my graduate degree, and step into a new chapter of my life—helping to impart to other athletes lessons I learned along the way. I knew my identity was not tied to being hired for my current position, but I was passionate about supporting others on their journey. When an individual understands who they are apart from sport, utilizes their resources with an attitude of gratitude, and lives a balanced life with their training, they are on the right path toward finding their freedom, which is key to reaching peak performance.

About the Author

Kristin Kaye was a member of the 2009 United States Rhythmic Gymnastics World Championships Group Team and US Senior Group National Team from 2007 to 2009. In 2000, she was a member of the US Junior Pan American Championships Group Team. In addition to her accomplishments as a group team member, Kristin was the 2002 US Junior National Champion and a member of the US Junior National Team from 2001 to 2002. Throughout her gymnastics career, Kristin had the opportunity to represent the United States at international competitions in Venezuela, Brazil, Canada, Germany, Bulgaria, France, Israel, Greece, Portugal, Spain, and Japan.

The significant gap between her major gymnastics accomplishments is due to the nearly four-year break she took from the sport in order to seek treatment for an eating disorder. Kristin's decision to return to the sport stemmed from the genuine passion she had for rhythmic gymnastics and the influence she hoped to have on younger athletes to show that this sport can be done in a healthy way. Kristin's comeback journey is something she has had the opportunity to share around the country for the past 15 years through various speaking engagements. Her story has been featured in Teen Magazine, the Chicago Tribune, and more. A full list of previous speaking engagements can be found on her website.

When Kristin later transitioned to rowing, she spent two seasons (2018 to 2019) on the Potomac Boat Club high performance sculling team in

Washington, DC. Kristin has her MS in psychology with an emphasis in sport psychology from California Southern University as well as her BA in psychology from Wheaton College. She currently lives in upstate New York, where she is honored to be supporting some of the nation's top athletes through the role of athlete life and programs specialist at the Lake Placid Olympic & Paralympic Training Center and hopes to combine her love of sport with her greatest desire of helping others see and embrace their own value, worth, and purpose in life.

Email: Kristinkaye12@gmail.com
Website: www.Kristin-kaye.com

Disclaimer: This material and the views and information in it are Kristin Kaye's own and presented on her behalf, not that of the USOPC or any of its members or affiliates; the material may not reflect their views or positions.

CHAPTER FIFTEEN
FROM PAIN TO THE PARALYMPIC PODIUM

By Jen Yung Lee
3x Paralympic Gold Medalist, Hockey; Army Veteran
San Antonio, Texas

The book is about developing a mindset for peak performance. There are numerous explanations on what that should be, and this is mine. It's not some type of universally applicable step-by-step guide that tells you what you need to do to become successful. For me, it's actually a story, the story of my life, and how its unpredictable challenges and curve balls gave me the mindset to compete and succeed at an elite level in my sport while also becoming who I am today.

The work is still in progress. There are numerous different types of pressure and situations that I haven't faced yet that will undoubtedly reshape me and my performance. Therefore, I cannot give you a "one-size-fits-all" mindset on what a true peak performance is or how to get there because it is different for everyone and life is ever-evolving. However, one thing I know for sure is that my mental health played, and will continue to play, a huge role along the way to my personal peak performance.

Fortitude and Suffering

My personal suffering began as early as third grade. I was born in Taipei, Taiwan, and have been involved in sports, starting as young as age three. From dribbling a basketball, participating in elementary track and field events, to being volunteered as my sister's hitting partner in badminton, I fell in love with all kinds of sports. One particular sport that I first got hooked on was baseball. That's when I knew I wanted to be an athlete. Not only was I hungry for the knowledge of the game, I was even hungrier to compete. My competitiveness in other sport activities picked up as well. However, everything changed in 1995. That's when I went from being one of the top athletes in my class, to my athletic attributes simply being erased from my identity when my family and I immigrated to the United States.

My naïve imagination of America, the land of the free, would soon be shattered when I first experienced racial bullying from my peers at my new American school. Normally, a FOB (fresh off the boat) kid like myself, a term which the "regular" English-speaking kids would have called us, would automatically get enrolled into an ESL (English as a Second Language) class and be in a classroom with other newly immigrated kids. However, I decided I wanted to go to a regular school and class at my grade level simply because the school had a baseball field. (Only later did I discover that all of the local elementary schools had baseball fields.)

So, there I was, enrolled in a classroom full of students that I had no idea how to communicate with because I did not speak a lick of English. Immediately, they knew I was a FOB, and the racial slurs and jokes about me being a FOB began to pour in on a daily basis. But, I didn't let it bother me. This is simply because I didn't understand what they were saying (I guess the jokes on them in the end). It was not until later, when my English began to improve, that I learned the terms "Chinaman," "chink," "slant eyes," "yellow monkey," and other racial slurs.

Eventually, none of these things mattered because the only things that mattered to me, at the time, were PE and recess. PE and recess were the only times I felt free and normal because I got to participate in all sorts of sports activities. I had no interest in learning any other subjects at school, so PE and recess were my safe havens, my therapy.

Sports eventually became my universal language to communicate with class-mates. It sounds cliché, but sports really are a universal language and unifying factor as seen many times in soccer. Although racial slurs would occur again from time to time, eventually I gained the respect of my classmates. Finally, I was no longer the kid who got picked last. Finally, I was no longer the kid who got picked last. Sports would eventually lead me to a lofty spot on the high school junior and varsity teams in basketball, track and field, baseball, and tennis.

Growing up, I learned to approach things one of two ways: first, out-work your competitor/opponent. Second, if the first fails, outsmart them. Unfortunately, like many other teenage kids in high school, my work ethic completely vanished as soon as I made the junior varsity team in basketball due to my ego, pride, and laziness.

After making the team, I felt like I was this "big hotshot" who didn't need to put in any more effort to improve my skills. The only sprints, jump shots, dribbling, or any other kind of training regiments I would perform were the required ones during team practices. This strategy didn't go well, and my beloved sanctuary of sports suffered through the end of my high school years. A couple of games before the end of our senior season, our head coach told us something that would forever be stuck in my mind: "Guys, for the majority of you, this may be the last time you will ever wear a jersey to represent something that is meaningful."

Trust Yourself by Trusting Others

Shortly after I graduated from high school, I enlisted in the US Army, effectively ending my athletic career by switching the jersey with a uniform. I enlisted in the military when I was only 18 years old, straight out of high school. I was a young kid, who was motivated and ready to learn with an open mind. But at the same time, I was a hothead in need of guidance, structure, and leaders that could teach me the value of leadership, teamwork, and discipline.

One thing I loved about the military, especially during basic training, was that they did not care about your social status. They didn't care whether you speak a different language or had a different cultural background because, to them, you are the same as everyone else. The army's objective is to mold you into a soldier by providing you the best resources they have to offer. So, either you get with the program, or "you're just a low dirty douchebag who will never do anything great in your life" (from a former drill sergeant. His words, not mine).

Once again, the universal language of sports and my natural athletic ability helped me excel in my military career. I graduated basic training with a distinguished honor of APFT of the training cycle. The Army Physical Fitness Test (APFT) consists of measuring the total number of pushups and sit-ups you can do in a two-minute span, followed by a timed two-mile run. I finished as the top APFT soldier of the cycle, and the result gave me accomplishment during graduation. Due to my athletic background and my high APFT score, I was fortunate to get into schools where I could endure the physical and mental challenge. This is also when I discovered the meaning of what work ethic is and how it could separate you from others who may also want to reach the same goal.

Overall, the military taught me how to trust my peers, comrades, teammates, and mainly, myself. The military showed me how to be a better teammate by understanding that you can never accomplish anything alone in this world, no matter how tough or easy the task. You may think you can do it all by yourself, but there is always someone (friend or foe) that will lend you a hand when you need it the most. Sometimes, you don't even notice it until later on down the road. So far in my life, I have not accomplished a single thing solely on my own. It's all been about the people helping me get to where I am today. The biggest challenge for most of us is whether we can trust ourselves by trusting others. This, of course, applies to achieving top levels in your sport as well.

Losing My Legs

On March 21, 2009, the Buddhist idea that "life is suffering" took on a whole new meaning to me. In Jacksonville, Florida, while riding my motorcycle along with four other colleagues from the military, I was struck by a vehicle when the driver failed to notice me in her blind spot. Two months later, I became an above-the-knee amputee, and my life changed forever. I didn't know if I could ever walk or run again, or even continue to serve my country. No one had any answers about whether or not I could still do any of those things. I began to lose hope as I sat and waited at home, recovering. Meanwhile, the army was trying to figure out what to do with me. I remember that as the lowest point of my life thus far. I had no idea what the true definition of being a disabled person really was until I actually became one.

Six months after my leg amputation, I was transferred to a military rehab facility called Center for the Intrepid (CFI) in San Antonio, Texas. As I slowly adjusted to being an amputee, the CFI gave me a whole different perspective and outlook on life. Prior to my transfer to the CFI, I really thought no one would ever understand what I was going through. No matter how much my family or friends tried to empathize, they would never understand how traumatic it was to me because all of their limbs are still intact.

I became very angry and depressed, and I was ready to give the middle finger to anyone I didn't want to talk to. But once I arrived at the CFI, I noticed there were at least a dozen amputees like me, who had either similar or worse injuries. You see, back in 2009, the US was still in the middle of combat operations in Iraq and Afghanistan. Since the country was still at war, there were many combat-wounded and injured service members. As I sat next to these combat wounded warriors, they gave me a quick glance and asked how my injury happened. For the first time since my accident, I could answer the question, "What happened to you?" without feeling like they were only asking out of sympathy. These wounded warriors didn't make any excuses to feel sorry for themselves. In fact, they embraced their injuries and continued the mission like they were trying to get back in the fight. During all of this, somehow I was able to reconnect with my childhood ambition in sports, and my competitive nature resurfaced as well.

Around October 2009, a combat-wounded veteran named Chris Leverkuhn was at the rehab facility asking if any patients wanted to try a new therapeutic sport called sled hockey. After attending sled hockey practices for several weeks, Chris asked if I was interested in playing on their travel team, which consisted of all military-wounded or injured service members from San Antonio.

"Wait, a travel-disabled sled hockey team?" I was thinking, "Who else out there would play this sport?" It turned out sled hockey had been around for a while, and there were a lot of great players out there who either played on the national team and represented their country at the Paralympic Games.

"Wait, the Paralympic Games? First of all, what's the Paralympics?" Those words and terms were all new to me, and I never thought anyone would take us, or disabled sports in general, seriously.

Acknowledge, Accept, and Embrace the Nerves

Nine months after getting into sled hockey for the first time, I went to Rochester, New York, to try out for the national sled hockey team along with two other teammates from San Antonio. The nerves immediately kicked in throughout the tryout weekend, but these types of nerves felt very familiar, reminding me of my childhood, my high school years, and even my time in the military when I was about to compete for a spot for the first time. One thing

I've learned is that nerves, anxiety, and pressure are something everyone will experience, regardless of what type of situation we put ourselves in. Whether it's a sports competition, job interview, public speaking, jumping out of a perfectly good airplane, taking a finals exam, or simply driving, you can never shake off these feelings. The more you practice, the more you prepare, and then the more confidence you will build to make yourself more comfortable. You will have better control of your nerves and a better understanding of how to handle that certain pressure when you encounter it.

For me, I can never shake off the nerves and pressure of wanting to throw up right before a game. Thus, I tend to have an empty stomach right before a game, and this gives me the edge to "play hungry" like a lion hunting for its prey. So, instead of resisting it or trying to hide it from my teammates or coaches, I've accepted my nerves, and I embrace the feeling of the puking sensation. The puking nerve will always be there, no matter what I do, but it makes me feel "locked in" and ready to go right after I puke.

To achieve your top-level athletic performance, I challenge you to embrace that uneasy feeling and let it happen. My puking nerves and the uneasy pressure led me to a spot on the national team and to many wins with my teammates as we played through the international exhibition matches, world championships, and my first Paralympic gold in Sochi, Russia.

When you feel on top of the world, you sometimes tend to forget the real reasons that got you there. As I mentioned earlier, my temperament was something that I had trouble controlling until later in 2018. After winning my first gold in 2014, I was going through a divorce while also dealing with the death of my mother. I was 27 years old, and I felt like I didn't owe anyone an explanation for anything that I did. So, instead of speaking to my coach or my general manager (GM) about what I was dealing with, I just left a simple text, notifying them I would not be playing in the upcoming season and I would return when I was ready.

When I was ready, I had to try out, and I was cut from the 2015 to 2016 national team. I didn't give up, and a year later, I was battling for a roster spot on the 2018 Paralympic Team. I got a call from the GM, notifying me that I actually made the 2018 Paralympic roster. I couldn't believe it and had to ask why they decided to go with me instead of someone else. The GM and the coaching staff from the national and development team all agreed that over the previous two years, I'd demonstrated my ability to not only become a better player but also I'd matured as an adult and as a leader on and off the ice. At the end of the day, I played well enough to redeem a spot on the team.

After winning my second gold medal with my teammates at the 2018 winter Paralympic games, I felt like I was on top of the world again. As we rolled into the 2018 to 2019 season, our winning streak continued when we won the world championship the following season. Our team was in shock when our goalie Steve Cash announced that he would be retiring due to personal reasons. The sudden retirement announcement shocked the entire sled hockey community because he was considered one of the all-time greats in the sport.

As I'd been the team's backup goalie, my GM informed me that I would be the starting goalie for the national team, "The net is yours now, Jen." Here I was, having been a backup goaltender for the last 11 seasons, and now suddenly I was the guy between the pipes for my team. I knew the biggest skill I needed to develop as a goaltender was mastering and refining my mental process.

"Dime-Size" Focus

I would soon learn how to be in the zone, how to "dime-size" focus like Steve Cash did when the opponent was tougher to win against. I only had two regular season games as a starting goalie before heading to the Paralympics. Those two games were against Canada, which I'd only faced twice as a starter before (one loss and one draw). When we lost the first out of the two exhibition matches, my mind was rattled more than ever. There were a lot of fundamental and mental mistakes that I personally thought I could've avoided. We ended up losing to Canada 4 to 3 because of my mental errors.

After losing in front of our home crowd, I felt like I totally let my team down with my performance. I had a hard time moving forward following that loss because I couldn't shake off the specific memory of when I let in a soft goal early in the third period and how that became the difference maker. I had trouble sleeping the same night after we lost because I began to question myself, "Am I even good enough to play at this level?" I began to have thoughts like, "Maybe I hid behind Steve's shadow far too long, and I'm used to him helping our team win in big situations."

The enlightenment finally set in when I accepted the fact that everyone makes mistakes, but it's up to me to see how tough I can respond and learn from the mistake. The first step is to overcome your personal aversion towards fear. You have to understand your failures and be prepared to face failure over and over again and the fear and discomfort that comes with it. You have to focus on the present moment and mentally know how to move forward from the past.

The following morning, after receiving a few words of encouragement from my teammates and my GM, my sense of enlightenment switched on. One thing I'd failed to do prior to the first game was mental preparation. I remember watching Steve during game days and how he mentally locked in by the time we had our pre-game meal. This "dime-size" focus doesn't start from puck drop. It starts from the time you wake up to play that day.

The Faceless Man with Inner Chi

In the second exhibition match, our team was ready to battle against Canada, and so was I. Not only did I stop smiling for the cameras before heading out on the ice, but the staying-loose, joking-around-with-my-teammates Jen Lee completely stopped as well. I focused more on the present moment by concentrating on my breathing. Breathing concentration helped my mind and my inner conscience to be more aware of the present moment, and the present moment only.

From the time we got on the ice during the pre-game warm-up, I became a faceless man. A faceless man means an emotionless person with no fear and doubt. A faceless man who was ready to face whatever was going to happen on the ice. A faceless man who isn't afraid of not being in control, who is ready to move forward quickly if he makes a mistake. There is no yesterday or tomorrow, and you're not afraid of the outcome, win or loss. It is only now, you can only control the present, the current shot, the current play, the current save, just like you are currently reading this. That was my mentality to reach my peak performance, and that was my inner chi, as I like to call it.

My inner chi came from all of my experiences from childhood, immigrating to the US, high school, military, the accident, rehabilitation, losses, wins, being cut, being a backup, becoming a starter, and many more that got me to that present moment. I wouldn't have discovered my inner chi without the practice of meditation and my study of Buddhism to process all of my past experience.

What separates a goaltender from an elite goaltender is the will to bounce back, the will to battle to the end for your teammates, the mental strength to take the losses and wins equally in stride. I knew how to play the game, but it was time to put it all together—mind, body, and spirit—to be an elite goaltender (which I haven't mastered, but I am getting better).

We ended up winning the second game, 4 to 1. It was my first win against Canada ever, and I dedicated that win personally to Steve Cash. Without his friendship, mentorship, and all of the battles we had during practices, I would've never understood what it takes to come to this level. Me backing him up and witnessing what he did best from my place on the bench for many years made me realize why he closed out tight games better than all other goaltenders out there. His mental attitude towards competitiveness and the will to win was contagious while, at the same time, also intimidating.

It Takes a Village, But in the End, It Is Up to You

A couple of months later, our team took another gold medal at the Winter Paralympics Games in Beijing, China. Nothing changed from the time I finally won my first game against Canada as a starter, to how I prepared for the Paralympics. Nothing changed in terms of my competitiveness, work ethic, and mental process because I also figured out what it takes to be a great teammate. Being a great teammate is always about working towards your craft, always striving to get better, and challenging yourself and your teammates to go outside of their comfort zone on and off the ice.

Use your ability to help others and always stay humble about what you currently have. Be grateful for how far the game has come, be grateful for the people that have helped you along the way to get to where you are, and leave the game better than when you started. It takes a love for the game and it also takes a village to help you attain peak levels of performance in sports, and it is entirely up to you to walk this path.

About the Author

Jen Yung Lee knows how to overcome adversity and create success. He is an Army Veteran and a three times Paralympic Gold Medalist in hockey who strives to make the world a better place. He's part of a veteran outreach program, he's a peer mentor, and he's a Para Goalie Coach.

Email: Horitiuslee@gmail.com
Instagram: @horay_shus
Twitter: @LifeofaLW
Facebook: Jen Yung Lee

CHAPTER SIXTEEN
UNLOCKING TRANSFORMATIONAL LEVELS OF PERFORMANCE

By Scott Macdonald
Founder, Peak Performance Coaching
Edinburgh, Scotland

There is one consistent question that every athlete I've worked with has asked me:

How do I unlock my next level of performance?

The answer is doing a 30/70 percent split between the following:

1. Improving technical execution (through practice, nutrition, etc.)
2. Freeing your mind

Every single top-level athlete (defined by those who are chasing one percent gains) has attributed the biggest gains they've had to the ability to free their mind, both in and out of competition.

If you focus on one thing, obsess about it, live it, breathe it, sleep it, then when that thing is going well, everything in life feels good. Life feels easy, you feel that your focus and sacrifices are being repaid. Everything feels a bit easier and worthwhile.

When that thing isn't going well, EVERYTHING can feel off—your confidence might dip, training becomes a grind, you might become grumpy, you might look for excuses or blame others, and/or you beat yourself up and question if you're really good enough. Life just starts to feel a bit harder.

The vast majority of athletes I work with are wrongly conditioned to knuckle down when it gets tough. They think they need to work harder, outwork the competition, focus more, reduce distractions, and immerse themselves in getting better at all costs. The problem is that it's often overwork that got them in the funk in the first place. Just buckling down and working harder is not what's going to get you *there* ... where you want to be.

My experience in working with elite sportsmen and sportswomen, CEOs, special forces operators, and those at the very top of their game has taught me that the higher you go, the more single-minded top performers can become. For the vast majority, that is what is blocking them from unlocking their potential.

For a long time, coaches have preached that single-minded focus is what it takes to get to the top, but we now know that's not true. It's old preaching based on a small minority of athletes who made it to the top, but definitely not the majority. If you look at those athletes that had that mindset, I'm sure you'll find behind that success, someone who chronically struggles with contentment and fulfilment. Behind those medals, trophies, and accolades is often a very empty and depressed individual. That's a big price to pay.

It's like in the '80s and '90s when training was about pushing yourself to the limit every day. This was thought to be the best way to get as fit as possible. It was easy to say and an easy mindset for people to buy into because there were a lot of athletes around describing their gruesome training regimes. Now we know that if you want to get the best out of your body, you have to let it recover. Sleep and rest are critical as is strengthening different parts of the body by doing cross-discipline training. The same is true if you want to maximise your mind's potential. And the mind is responsible for at least 50 percent of your performance. If it's not firing on all cylinders, it doesn't matter how well conditioned your body is, you will not reach anywhere near your potential.

Think of it like this: if you're building a Lego tower and you build it straight up with just one square block on top of another. It doesn't take long until you see you can't add any more blocks; otherwise, it'll fall. Or a slight "lean" starts, and you freeze in the hope you don't make it fall.

That's what it's like with elite performers. Often, they focus so intently on one thing that they can very quickly build a very high tower, but then one of two things happens:

1. They hit a plateau and can't go any higher (doesn't matter how many Lego bricks you have available, you just can't put them on).
2. Their confidence and/or performance takes a hit and everything feels "off" (the Lego tower leans or falls).

There isn't an elite performer that I've ever worked with who hasn't experienced this. But here's the interesting thing. The answer is not—double-down, refocus, remove distractions, and work harder.

The answer is—build a tower next to you. When the main tower starts to lean, it has another tower to support it. When your performance in your chosen sport is a bit off, there's something else in your life that is going well and helps to support you. There's another tower to support the main tower. You realise, "Yes, it's frustrating that I'm not getting my optimal performance right now, but the other things in my life are actually going really well", so your confidence and focus don't drop as much. That one-off poor result all of a sudden doesn't feel like a sucker punch to the stomach.

You can stay happy.

You can stay motivated.

Then, when you're standing on the start line, crossing the white line, or teeing up the ball, when the pressure starts cranking up and the anxiety starts to peak, you can relax a bit because you realise there's more to life than just this. *This moment is really important, and I should definitely have all of my focus on it, but I know that if it doesn't work out, my tower doesn't come crashing down. It just leans slightly or the tallest piece may come off, but then I'm building from a stronger foundation.*

Having a strong foundation makes it safer to fail and ensures failure is just a small dip, not a crash to the bottom.

Ever hit a plateau but been too scared to try something new? If you make the wrong decision, the consequences feel like they could be catastrophic. That's because if your life is built around a single tower and it does fall, the impact is very large. But if you have other focuses in life, change is less scary.

With the Lego analogy, you can use two-block pieces, three-block pieces, four-block pieces, five-block pieces or even six-block pieces. You can try new things. And the wider the Lego bricks you use, the tighter and stronger the tower becomes.

Think of the greatests of all time (GOATs) and how they've done it. Michael Jordan—golf. Jordan handled the pressure cooker environment of being basketball's GOAT by playing golf almost every chance he got. He was a single-figure handicapper and to this day plays five times a week. He also loved learning business and became one of Nike's greatest ever ambassadors because it wasn't just a sponsorship deal for him, he loved learning business.

Usain Bolt had music, clubbing, and video games. Bolt knows when things aren't going his way, he has these other areas in his life that bring him great joy. Some might argue that they aren't "complimentary" to being an athlete, but that's just lazy and naïve. They help him relax, switch off, and reset. Every athlete must have these to turn to if they want to be able to reach the top. Mohammed Ali was a civil rights activist. Serena Williams, a fashion designer. The list is endless. They were all able to adapt, find new levels, and consistently succeed because their lives were about more than just their chosen profession.

People think sportsmen and women are different because their "job" is something they love, and while many of you would agree (especially in a public setting), far more of you tell me that it very often does feel like a "job" a lot of the time.

Have you ever heard of a rich investment manager who put all their money into one company's shares? No. Because the first thing you ever learn in investing is to diversify. Always have more than one stock because, at some point, it will definitely go down, so you need the other stocks to prop up your portfolio.

I hope you're starting to get the point.

So step 1—find something else to focus on other than your primary sport. Something else that lights a fire inside you and brings you peace. It might be golf, it might be knitting, it might be art, or it might be virtual reality gaming. Everyone has their own thing, but it must be something you're passionate about. Don't just think of something that was a hobby a few years ago and seems obvious or something that you've always wanted to try. It has to be something that you really look forward to and you rush to get to because you don't want to miss time spent doing it. That will focus your mind and body on it.

Now if you've gotten this far, you might be thinking some of this is counterintuitive and not what's been drummed into you for the last X years, but there's clearly something switching a light on in your mind. That's what I always see in the athletes I work with that truly reach the top. They're willing to go off the beaten track. Their desire to be the best means they know they can't be like everyone else, so they seek out alternative ways of building their tower higher than anyone else. The very best, do the things that terrify them. The things that take them completely out of their comfort zone. Because in that space is the greatest opportunity for growth.

One percent improvements are found in doing the things you're already doing, but doing them a little bit better. Ten-fold improvements are found in doing the things that you've never done before.

Every athlete is searching for that moment when everything clicks, it all seems effortless, you see things in slow motion, you see what your opponent is going to do before they even know it themselves. Every fibre in your body is focussed on executing, and they're in perfect harmony with one another. You are completely present in that moment. This moment, or period, is called a state of flow. Many chase it, few truly experience it.

Of all the athletes I've worked with, when we've started working together, less than 10 percent could recall it lasting any longer than a fleeting moment or series of moments in a game. A boxer described it as lasting "90 seconds of a 12-round fight." A tennis player described it as two games in a five-set match. Very few could articulate it as a state of mind they had for the full day.

Now imagine if you woke up on the day of your race, match, etc., and everything you did went perfectly. The sun was shining, your shower was at the perfect temperature, your clothes felt and looked epic. You started your pre-race ritual and everything felt strong but relaxed, explosive but calm, fluid but disciplined. How did you get into that state?

Was it because you were focussed on nothing else but the race? Quite possibly in that moment, but it's unlikely that's what you were doing in the weeks leading up to it. Was it because you visualised nothing but success? Possibly, but even if you focus on the process and not the outcome, that often becomes all-consuming and overwhelming.

The answer is that you probably subconsciously acknowledged that you had done everything that had been asked of you by your coach, nutritionist, psychologist, and every other member of your team. And this gave you a sense of freedom.

And, therefore, flow (because flow = freedom).

Chasing flow is extremely difficult, but chasing freedom is a lot easier. Freedom comes from knowing you've done everything you could have done AND knowing that whatever happens, you will be okay. If you win, you'll be okay. If you come second, you'll be okay. If you come last, you'll be okay.

Imagine how differently you'd approach not just your race day, but how differently you'd approach your life if you had that sense of freedom. And that's why you need to start visualising *not* winning.

Boom!—I said it. Let that sit there for a minute and ask yourself, "How does that sit in my head?"

If it scares the hell out of you, then good. That's exactly why you need to do it. The next level sits on the other side of fear. Every breakthrough you've ever had came in your greatest moments of fear.

Experience tells me that with visualisation, you need to spend approximately 80 percent of your time visualising the perfect process (not outcome); ten percent on how you will react if the unwanted happens, e.g., your competition posts a world record just before you're due to race or your bike has a puncture halfway through the race; and 10 percent on how you're going to be if this doesn't work out how you thought it would.

It's in that 10 percent that freedom exists because then you can truly break away from your life being defined by that moment and know that whatever happens, your life is still going to be amazing. Imagine how much more enjoyable training would be, how much more relaxed game or race day would be if you turned up with absolute 100 percent confidence that whatever happens, you are still going to be great. Win or lose. You won't be a failure, you won't be ashamed, you won't have missed out on that sponsorship deal, you won't have missed out on a gold medal. You'll be someone who gave their absolute all and you're excited about what's next. Imagine the freedom you'd compete in … and you know it's in that space that your best performances are achieved.

Visualise yourself coming second or last, whatever it may be to you. Close your eyes. Then picture being given a stunning box, glowing, wrapped up in gold with a beautiful bow on it. You're handed it by a spirit that floats to you as if from another world. There are clouds around you, and you're receiving the most beautiful gift in the most amazing environment you have ever seen. Inside that box is the key to your next level. It tells you what you need to do next. It might be a technical improvement, a nutritional change, a tweak to your preparation routine, or it might be that you need to change to an entire new phase in your life. The answer will be found from your own self-reflection and team discussions, but that gift is there every single time things don't go perfectly.

Now you're not visualising failure. You're actually preparing yourself for the next level of performance. And you're doing it with complete and utter freedom. You have a new energy in training, you have a new focus, a new enthusiasm for friends and families. In this space you manifest great things, sponsors are attracted, new connections and new opportunities arise, and you're reinvigorated to grab them all with both hands. They're no longer distractions. They're building blocks to build your tower higher. You're diversifying your portfolio to make it as strong as possible.

Michael Jordan knew it. Usain Bolt knew it. Serena Williams knew it. It's how the greats are created. Now it is your turn to know this, use this, and allow your peak performance as an athlete to flow in the successes of winning and being a winner regardless of the outcome.

About the Author

Scott MacDonald is one of the world's leading performance coaches. He's worked with some of the best athletes, CEOs and entrepreneurs on Earth, and it's this variety of minds and experience that enables him to unlock transformational levels of performance. He's based in Scotland where he lives with his wife and two children.

Email: scott@scottmaccoaching.com
Website: www.scottmaccoaching.com

CHAPTER SEVENTEEN
YOU ARE A PEAK PERFORMER

By Kurt Madden
Founder, TriPrime; Ironman Competitor since 1980
San Diego, California

I had no skin on my heels. There were 65 miles remaining. It was 2013, and I was in Silverton, Colorado, for the Hardrock 100, a 100-mile trail run that requires 33 thousand feet of hill climbing, as well as 33 thousand feet of hill descents. And then, of course, all participants must cross waist-deep streams.

When the race began, the skin on my feet was intact. But 25 miles in, my support crew had to cut off three inches of skin on both of my heels in order to remove the blisters that had formed. The expectation was that I'd no longer continue.

Quitting begets quitting. So, too, does success beget success. Peak performers have learned to search for joy in the journey. And that is why I stayed in the race. Every step was agony. When you have no skin on your heels, the pain is not dull. But peak performers know how to chunk the seemingly impossible into smaller bites that just might be manageable. Each "small bite," whether it consists of making it to the next tree, or to the top of the next ridge, is a win. Each win earns a reward, the release of dopamine in your brain, and this creates momentum. It is this momentum that enabled me to finish the Hardrock 100 in just shy of 40 hours.

Little did I realize how growing up in a dysfunctional home, in the inner city of San Diego, California, would provide me with a foundation for peak performance. Peak performers need adversity or stress, challenges or obstacles.

Peak performers need these things so that they can refine their "fight." In the dilemma that presents as fight or flight, peak performers learn to lean into a fight.

I leaned into my first fight when I was five. I was diagnosed with a heart abnormality, and the cardiologist told my father that I should not go outside to play, as I was only expected to live for six more months. I remember looking out the window. My friends were all playing outside. I just sat alone in my room and watched. After one month of this torture, my father made an appointment with another cardiologist, and he too agreed that I had a heart abnormality, but instead of prescribing "flight," he suggested I fight. He recommended that I get outside, play, and do what I can to make my heart stronger. That day, I received my first lesson in peak performance. No longer would I shy away from the problem and allow it to determine my path. From that day forward, I leaned into problems, knowing that with a combination of hard work, passion, curiosity, and grit, I could determine my own path. This is what peak performers do.

And what is most exciting is that anyone can learn how to become a peak performer. Like any ability, it requires comprehension and realization. We must become students of the process, and we must practice regularly. Doing so can help us consistently turn adversity into excellence. It can turn a mishap into momentum. It can position us for regular biochemical rewards in the form of serotonin and dopamine, the good neurotransmitters that give us the drive and ambition we need to perform optimally.

When teaching peak performance, I focus on four things: mindset, Kaizen, grit, and scheduling the finish. Let's look at each of these in turn.

Mindset

The proper mindset can be a major contributor to being a peak performer. When your mind and body are working together in the athletic arena, this synergistic feeling and phenomenon can give you a huge return on your investment. It is often referred to as the "growth mindset" where challenges are embraced. Conversely, the wrong mindset or attitude can put you into a death spiral. This "fixed mindset" does not embrace or lean into challenges; instead, it shrinks when challenged, morphing the peak performer into a non-completer.

In 2015, one day before the Ironman World Championship in Kailua, Kona, Hawaii, I was returning to shore from an open-water swim, and I stepped on a spiny sea urchin. I was barefoot. I felt the pain of tiny poisonous harpoons piercing the thin, sensitive flesh of my foot. In 18 hours, I was supposed to swim 2.4 miles in the ocean, bike 112 miles through the lava fields, and run 26.2 miles through heat, humidity, and the Natural Energy Lab, a special section of the Big Island where temperatures reach 130 degrees.

Now, if I had a fixed mindset, I'd have decided not to race in the World Championship. I'd have concluded that my chances were no longer optimal. I'd have found an excuse to hide behind. Fortunately, I have learned how to adopt a growth mindset, which means that I embrace challenges, choosing to persist in the face of setbacks. Those who've raced the Ironman World Championship know that physical ability is important; however, without the appropriate mindset, peak performance is not an option. I have learned that peak performers are able to keep a sustained focus on mentally grinding longer and harder than they thought they could, all the while visualizing themselves finishing strong, not giving up. The takeaway is this: the more you utilize the proper mindset over an extended period of time, the more the odds will increase that you can do it again and again and again.

Kaizen

"Kaizen," continuous improvement in small sequential steps, can be achieved by anyone who is chasing an athletic dream, goal, or experience that will bring them joy and fulfillment. Kaizen is an important principle that will allow you to be a peak performer. The next time you go into a Trader Joe's and are checking out, the attendant will often ask you if you found everything. You might respond, "Yes, I did; however, I could not find the Kaizen." You should get an immediate response because this is one of the core values of Trader Joe's. As a peak performer, you need to get Kaizen into your DNA and visualize yourself continuously improving. Adopting Kaizen in my professional life and throughout my athletic endeavors keeps me focused, engaged, and striving for excellence.

Grit

Peak performers are gritty. They work really hard to follow through on a commitment, and they have a sound work ethic. Acquiring grit takes time. It may take several years. Some people seem to have an innate ability to be gritty.

However, grit can be taught. In the world of athletics, grit will provide you with the tenacity and resilience to be a top finisher and/or tap into your full potential. You develop grit through adversity, insurmountable obstacles, and having the inner confidence to focus on your mission and complete the task. Students of peak performance can deliberately schedule daily opportunities for "grit practice."

Looking back on my life, I firmly believe that growing up in a dysfunctional home in the inner city provided me with multiple opportunities to develop grit, earning me the nickname, "Mad Dog," as I used my stamina and grit to finish strong and find ways to come out on top. Even now, at age 66, I make sure that "grit practice" is on my calendar. It serves as a daily reminder that adversity is non-negotiable, that when we find ourselves in a dark place, we don't flee. We lean in, we stick with it, we believe in ourselves, and we employ positive self-talk until we reach excellence.

Schedule the Finish

What does it mean to schedule the finish? You start by doing some backward mapping and going through everything you need to ensure you get yourself across the finish line and finish strong. Some people tend to forget about the importance of getting your ducks lined up to ensure you are in full control, both mentally and physically, at the end of a workday, a business meeting, a training session, or a competition. The feeling and gratitude you experience when you finish strong are second to none. I often say, it is not always important how you start an event; it is more important to focus on how you finish.

I have competed four times in the Ultraman World Championship on the Big Island of Hawaii, so I know how demanding the 52.4-mile double-marathon can be on day three. That's why, in preparation for this phase of the race, I dedicate time to visualizing the last 13 miles. I identify landmarks and cues. I list what is required to finish strong. I deliberately train on this final portion of the course so that when I get to this point in the actual race, I know that I've been there before and that I've done it successfully. It gives me a huge advantage over my competitors. It builds the inner confidence necessary to fight until the end.

Scheduling the finish can be applied to finite games (like meeting Q1 targets or winning the Ultraman World Championship), and it can also be applied to infinite games. For instance, when scheduling the finish of your life, it is imperative to ask yourself, "How do I want to be remembered?" and "Will I leave a legacy of peak performance?" The answers have the potential to minimize regret and to reinforce how you will be remembered. You can inspire your family, friends, and others to be peak performers, which simply means you embraced the challenges of life, performed at the highest level possible, and every day you woke up a with fire in your belly and passion in your heart to be the best craftsman you could be with the tools you were given and the skills you developed along the way.

Many people reach out to me about how to achieve peak performance, and one of my most common responses is that every single day is an opportunity to practice your craft. Take the first step to overcome inertia, engage with the sport that you love, and strive toward execution and perfection from start to finish. And when you have to push, when you have to dig deep, embrace it with the inner confidence to give it your best. Make sure to remind yourself: "I was born to do this, so let me make sure I do it well." Every single day is an opportunity to experience excellence and continuous improvement in your quest for achieving a lifetime filled with peak performances.

About the Author

As a professional triathlete, Kurt Madden finished three times in the top ten at the Ironman World Championship. A world-class trail runner and USA Track and Field 24-Hour Champion, Kurt set the national record for running 200 miles in 48 hours. He is the two-time winner of the Ultraman World Championship and 2019 Inductee into the Ultraman World Championship Hall of Fame. From 2017 to 2021, Kurt was the #1 ranked Age Group Male in the Ironman All World Athlete Rankings. In 2021, Kurt was the four-time North American Age Group Ironman Champion. Kurt is an Ironman Certified Coach, USAT Certified Coach, TriDot Coach, and is currently the CEO/President of KM Educational Consulting and Executive Coaching Services.

Email: kurt@kmeducationalconsultant.org
Facebook: TriPrime LLC

CHAPTER EIGHTEEN
YOUR BIGGEST RIVAL IS ALWAYS YOURSELF

By Akari Nakahara
Figure Skating Coach, 2x Int'l Championship Medalist
Los Angeles, California

The crowd cheers and the lights shine, the cameras roll, and the whole world watches. From a young age, you have been preparing for, dreaming about, and striving for this moment. You perform the best performance of your life. However, this performance was not enough to make it to the Olympics, your ultimate goal. You know you gave it your best shot, and you realize that this dream can only be achieved by a handful of incredible athletes. You did everything you could. You should hold your head up high for that. In the bottom of your heart, however, tears are flowing like the Nile River. At times you find yourself wondering, "Why am I here? What is the meaning of my life? Have I been training all these years to become a nobody?"

If your mind is constantly spiraling into a dark, soulless, never-ending chasm of negativity, I am here to help you. Today I am writing to remind you that we are all somebody. We are all here for a reason. There is a unique life for each of us in this universe that is different from that of everyone else. There is no such thing as an easy life; no one's life is. Each of us encounters challenges, hardships, and difficulties regularly. But, hey, that's what keeps life fascinating. That is what makes us better people; not yesterday, maybe not today or tomorrow, but in the days, weeks, months, and years to come. Make your life interesting by adding your own twist. Your biggest rival is always yourself. Let me explain to you why that is.

Your Mind Is Your Best Friend

Your mind is like your best friend. It follows you wherever you go, whatever you do. On the days you get along well, things start coming together nicely. Everything turns out just the way you wanted, and it's all happily ever after. On the days when you are fighting a battle against your mind, everything goes south. As your bestie slams you into a cold sheet of ice, you resist, but to no avail, and rather the situation escalates. Both of you get frustrated, drown in the deep icy waters, and the day's plans are ruined.

This is what happens when your mental and physical states do not cooperate. Do you think that there is nothing you could do under these circumstances? If you find yourself thinking this, then try thinking further. You are capable of bringing integrity between your mind and body. You are the only person in this world that can make that possible. Not me, not your parents, instructors, peers, or boss. Although you may be influenced by outside sources, you are the sole one controlling your inner mind, body, and life. What could you do to start guiding your mind towards the correct winding path up the mountains of success and glory?

Believe in Yourself

One word I love in the English dictionary is "believe." We use this word in phrases such as "believe in yourself," "I believe I can do it," and "Believing is important." Have we thought of what it means to "believe" in yourself or others? Believing means accepting something as true. That is something to take to heart because if you believe in something, one day it may become true under the right circumstances. If you have a career goal, try saying it out loud or writing it down. Talk to yourself in the affirmative. "I believe that I can do this. I believe that I can make this happen." Never talk negatively to yourself, such as, "I can't do this," "I am not talented enough," or "It's too difficult." When we talk to ourselves positively, it makes our mind think positively as well.

YOUR BIGGEST RIVAL IS ALWAYS YOURSELF

In one of my favorite songs, "Hero," by the top-selling artist Mariah Carey, there is a verse that goes, "So when you feel like hope is gone/ Look inside you and be strong/ And you'll finally see the truth / That a hero lies in you."

Everybody has some days when they feel desperate and hopeless, and that is okay. Just do not give in to those feelings. Stay strong. Believe in yourself, and tell yourself that everything will be alright tomorrow. That dream of yours may not be true today, but it may be someday. That pure light of hope is what propels our mind and body to start working together to achieve our goals.

Learn from Your Mistakes

As an elite figure skater in training for over 17 years, I have learned that making a mistake is not a disastrous thing. It is not the end of the world. Every time I fell on the ice, the more chances I got to get back up and become stronger. No matter how hard I fell, at practice or competition, I never gave up. As long as I knew that those mistakes gave me opportunities to reflect and grow upon myself, I did not regret making those mistakes. I perceive every mistake as a learning opportunity. They are stepping stones for me to utilize when launching myself closer to my ultimate goals. Even the most experienced elite athletes make mistakes, and that is nothing to be ashamed of. Although sometimes these mistakes may seem irreparably damaging to your career, combat those negative thoughts. Let out your inner positivity, and gradually but surely, make it more powerful.

Picture your entire athletic career you'd like to pursue as a painting on a large canvas. A minor mistake or mishap you make is a mere speck made with a flick of a paintbrush on that canvas. With effort, dedication, goals, and other valuable factors, you can overpaint that speck. Without learning from our past mistakes, we cannot flourish.

Many athletes fear making mistakes and admitting to them. I have seen so many athletes find excuses and run away from what is laid out in front of them. Reality is harsh, it is never easy for anyone. If it appears that "one athlete" made it to the elite level without any hardships, you are just making assumptions. They too have most likely had extremely difficult times at one point in their career. What separates them from others is that they had the positive mindset and determination to bring themselves up from the darkest pits. They made every effort they could to crawl back up into the shining light.

"You Can Achieve Anything If You Try"—Is This True?

It's no secret that I'm an avid athlete driven by a strong motivation to achieve my career goals. I am a strong believer in seasonal planning and goal setting. Setting short- and long-term goals, and having the determination to make those goals a reality is critical in sports and life alike. The deep motivation I have has given me the strength and grit to train harder. As a young athlete aspiring to be something significant, I believed in the mantra, "If you work hard, you can achieve whatever you set your mind to." The harder you work, the greater the reward. I learned that this is partially true, but not entirely.

Throughout my competitive figure skating career, I had the ultimate dream of becoming an Olympian. As I accomplished goal after goal, year after year, I thought that my efforts and commitments to the sport would someday bring me to that dream stage. Unfortunately, this lofty dream of mine will remain a fantasy, as I carry on in my athletic career. Now, as a coach of many young athletes working hard and pursuing the same big dream as I did, I am grateful for the experiences and opportunities I had growing up.

I have read in so many books, seen in movies, and heard from successful elite athletes that all of their long-term goal accomplishments came solely from the effort. That miracles do happen as long as you give it your all. Of course, I want to believe that achieving milestones in sports is this simple. If it were a simple mathematical equation of "effort = result," we'd all be Olympic gold medalists because everybody gives their maximum effort.

Sadly, sports are much more complicated. The energy you put into your training is just one of the many significant controllable variables that ultimately lead up to results. Other controllable variables come into play, such as equipment maintenance, body care, technique, and mind setting. On top of these, many uncontrollable variables are also at play, and they are factors athletes have no control over. Some uncontrollable variables include the performance of another competitor, the condition of the competition arena, and the timing of available opportunities.

For example, in figure skating, I have seen many elite skaters miss the opportunity to compete at the Olympics because of the exquisite timing of the four-year Olympic cycle. Despite being in top shape the previous year, they miss out on the Olympics the following year due to changes in their body physique or injuries sustained during training. Only the athletes that have all of those controllable and uncontrollable factors in their favor at the exactly right moment make it to that Olympic stage.

Although we all want to believe the saying that effort is all you need to win, sports are much more complex. Even with this complexity, as I mentioned earlier, having faith in yourself is key. As soon as you stop believing in yourself, you will fall apart.

In this fast-paced sports environment, factors are constantly changing around you. Daily athletes make every endeavor they can to adapt to these changes and the environment set for them. Out of millions of athletes with strong motivation, belief, and determination, only a handful make the cut. It may seem unfair and cruel at times. Many athletes quit pouring in the toil when they realize that it isn't enough. I fancy that this harsh reality is what makes our careers more demanding, more rewarding, and more interesting. Those with a strong mindset have a great advantage when barging through the doors of hardship.

Winning Isn't Just About the Results

As I see it, everyone is a winner. By checking off your practice lists, participating in a competition without any injuries, or simply telling yourself, "I tried my best, and that is what matters," you're already a winner. Know that performance results and gold medals themselves do not define who you really are. Rather, it is the years of diligent work, dedication, sweat, and tears that define your true values. Of course, everybody longs to hang that massive 556-gram Olympic gold medal around their neck. Everybody wishes to enjoy the views of the world from the top of that same podium. Despite our yearnings, we also need to accept that not everything will go as planned.

Shape your mindset towards the positive. See your small daily achievements as fragments of a larger accomplishment. If you are not able to reach that ultimate career goal in the long run, look back at all of those smaller accomplishments you've made. This is your very own journey that you've carved to this date. There are many things that you should proudly hold your head up high for. Value and cherish every moment you've been blessed to experience. Not everybody has had the same experiences and opportunities as you.

No matter how hard we try not to be jealous of others, as humans, we all have that envy deep inside us. "That person achieved something remarkable. I wish I was that person." However, many people in this world would also think the same of you. They'd wish to have walked in your shoes and accomplished what you have. Everybody has their own story, and that is what makes us unique. Every human being is amazing. You cannot determine a person's true value by looking at their results from a single competition or career accomplishment; you must look deeper into their souls.

Be Mindful of What Is the Most Important

What I would like all of you to take home today is not a gold medal. Instead, I hope you all take home safe and happy thoughts. A comfortable and safe environment in which your mind can do lots of diligent work. Even though a home may seem to have been destroyed in a hurricane, it can always be rebuilt. If you need help rebuilding your home, ask the people you love for their help. You do not have to fight this all alone. No matter how many times you fall, you will get back up.

Today, you will start guiding your mind on the long road to inner victory. You will always win against your yesterday. Be proud. Be modest and humble. Be appreciative. And, most importantly, be yourself.

About the Author

Akari Nakahara is a six-year Team USA and International Selection Pool (ISP) ladies singles figure skater. A six-time International Skating Union (ISU) international competitor representing Team USA and two-time ISU international medalist. A five-time US Figure Skating National Championships competitor and two-time US National Championships medalist. Her first ISU international assignment representing Team USA was at age 12.

Akari's name is engraved on trophies held at the US Figure Skating Hall of Fame. She is a member of the US Figure Skating Scholastic Honors Team, received the USFSA Graduating Seniors Platinum Award, Athlete Alumni Ambassador (3A) Award of US Figure Skating, and is a two-time USFSA Memorial Fund Recipient. Akari is a US Figure Skating and Professional Skaters Association Rated licensed coach and US Figure Skating Triple Gold Medalist. She's a member of the USFSA Athlete Advisory Committee, Tests Committee, Programs and New Programs Development Committee, State Games Subcommittee, SafeSkate Committee, and High School Programs Subcommittee..

Email: akarinakahara@hotmail.com
Website: https://www.linkedin.com/in/akarinakahara

CHAPTER NINETEEN
BECOMING A SUCCESS

By Solly Nowrozi
Pro Squash Athlete; Founder, I&B Investment Co.™
Brisbane, Australia

The person you become attracts all the things in your life.
—Jim Rohn

As a visionary, I always had a vision to be a successful athlete and a successful entrepreneur. However, when my family moved to Australia as an immigrant and was living in a high-crime, unsafe, low-income and rough environment with people consuming drugs, alcohol, and with no vision in life, my desire was to live with my family in a safe, affordable, and successful environment to give me a chance to succeed in my life and to change the course of my legacy.

I was once quite religious and grew up in a religious community. What I experienced was that others in my community were small-minded and jealous. They were always on the lookout for someone on whom they could be a negative influence, someone whose vision and hope they'd try to destroy.

What happened is that I started to question my beliefs and my entire being because I never felt good about the religion I was following. I never had a sense of peace and belonging. I found that the religious environment was negative. There was too much hard discipline regarding seemingly petty matters. I often felt disturbed.

When some of the religious community members heard about my success as an athlete, they commended my efforts and congratulated me for my success. One evening the head of the community asked me to send him my biography. As I was a highly successful athlete in the game of squash, both in our community as well as in all Australia back then, this person claimed he'd use the biography to petition the local Member of Parliament (MP) to get me some grant money that would fund my participation in a squash tournament that I desperately wanted to play in.

Since I was quite young at the time, I accepted. I was super excited at the possibility of receiving the funding because it was taxing working on my own to raise the money. I was working at a squash club, cleaning the courts and dirty toilets, and at the same time I was training full-time and attending school. Besides my training, I never liked any of the things that I was doing, but because my family didn't have the financial capabilities to support me in squash tournaments, I had to work at the club to support my goals in squash.

To clarify, I love my family unconditionally and everyone else who supported me because without them, I wouldn't be where I am now.

One evening, I got some news from my elder brother. He came to me and said, "These guys are ripping you off. They are using you to get the grant for themselves and the community!"

When I heard that, I was furious. I decided right then that I had enough of them. I went with my brother and told them that I wasn't going ahead with the grant, and they needed to cancel my application immediately. To my surprise, they did so because I said that I would contact the local Member of Parliament myself to reveal their dirty agenda.

Boy, that felt good—standing up for myself and my rights.

Ultimately, they cancelled my application, and I never interacted with them again.

I always had the belief that miracles are born in every adversity. In the moment of adversity, it is hard to see the miracle, but you will always find it. I can guarantee you that. One of the miracles that was born in this adversity was me getting to number seven in the World Juniors Ranking in 2015. I must mention how grateful I am to my entire family, my coaches, mentors, and everyone else who supported me.

The key for me to be ranked number seven in the world was my determination, my clear goal, and my mission. I persevered through thick and thin and kept my spirit alive. The secret is to never quit. Always show up, taking actions and committing.

In addition, the second miracle that came from that adverse situation was me leaving my community, religion, and its beliefs.

After years of researching and being curious to find out how I could reach the success level that every athlete and entrepreneur aims for, I finally found out what success is. The following is what I've learned:

1. Success is striving and progressively working towards an idea, ideal, vision, mission, or goal.
2. Success is what you become, not what you look to achieve.

The more I contemplate the ideas of achieving peak levels of success as an athlete and beyond, the more my consciousness expands, and I see infinite abundance and success in my mind's eye. As I hustle and work every day on my businesses, I&B Investment Co.™ and Regal Silk™, and as I further develop my being, I realize that to achieve success in my life, I must become that successful version of myself. How to do that? The answer: SELF-IMAGE. I find that your self-image is the key to you becoming a success and attracting success in your life.

It is through building your self-image, you can heal illness, become an Olympic athlete, build a multi-billion-dollar business, etc. It's fascinating, right?

The next question is—what can you do to build a self-image? My answer—sit in a quiet room all by yourself, take a blank sheet of paper, and contemplate these questions:

1. What is my vision and mission in life?
2. What value can I add to my family, my community, my country, and the world?
3. What do I have to become to achieve my vision and mission?

Respond to these questions, writing in the present tense and in detail. Be crystal clear with everything. Also, remember that even though you might be doing this exercise with the aim for achieving peak performance in your sport, your vision and mission is the desire that you are looking to attract in life. It is the end desired result. Most importantly, write down the date you want to achieve your vision and mission. Make your vision and mission as big as you want and think big.

This brings me to the second part of becoming a success and attracting the success you truly deserve and desire.

Take two more sheets of paper. Write down all your goals on one page and your targets for reaching those goals on the second page. Remember that a goal is something long-term, anything that can take a year or more to achieve. A target for reaching a particular goal (similar to a milestone) can be hourly, daily, weekly, fortnightly, monthly, three-monthly, six-monthly, and such.

When writing your goals and targets, make sure that you cover all areas of life (beyond just your sport), such as self-development, health, relationships, finance, business, community, etc. Write every goal that comes to your mind, and write them in the present tense. Also, be sure to write "thank you, thank you, thank you" and the current day's date on the paper. Whilst doing these exercises, it is critical that your targets and goals are in line with your vision and mission, so check that out and make adjustments as necessary.

After this, pick 12 of the goals that you really want to attract and describe each of those 12 goals in detail. Remember, the 12 goals are the most important ones from your list, which covers all the areas of your life. To describe each of these 12 most important goals in detail means you would give the projected date of achievement, the color, the type, the flavor, the smell, etc. (getting all your senses involved) of each one.

The idea for these exercises is to help you get very clear on your vision, mission, goals, and targets, with the more important aim of helping you see yourself as your most successful version. This is more than just scribbling on paper. See it as—*you are writing miracles of your life with your own hands, which get manifested in your life now.*

As the great artist Vincent Van Gogh once said, "I dream my painting and then I paint my dream." This saying has really stuck with me because it is very true. Whether achieving peak levels of performance as an athlete or as a businessperson, everything starts in the mind and with the vision before it's manifested. I will take this even further by saying the following:

1. In your mind, visualize your desired vision and mission.
2. Expect and feel it strongly that you've already attracted your desired vision and mission.
3. By writing it down, you start the manifestation of the desired vision and mission.
4. By bringing your spirit, mind, and body in line, you are materializing your desired vision and mission.

Now for the third and final aspect of becoming and attracting the success you desire in your life—you must commit to your vision and mission and take daily actions. The reason being, without commitment and daily actions, you are not doing your part.

Think of it like this—you plant the seed (your idea), cultivate it, nurture it, guard it, and then the time to harvest will come. The law also suggests that there is always a season for sowing and reaping. So, be very careful what you plant in your mind. Keep that positive mental attitude, focus your mind on your desired vision and mission, expect goodness, and take daily actions. The reason I'm emphasizing the action part is because when we act, we are getting to work, so the miracle can happen. The miracle is that invisible force that gathers all around us, pulling and attracting the circumstances and opportunities that are aligned with our vision and mission and moving us with momentum towards it.

A final insight, which I consider a life secret, each of us is a spiritual being, having a brief experience in this world in our human body, which is a vehicle; our name, gender, race, status, etc., are all labels, which we get and experience in this realm of life. Whilst we are all going to leave this brief world and our spirit will one day travel to that infinite place, filled with goodness and abundance, I urge you to love others and be kind to others. Take care of your spirit, mind, and body, and help others do the same.

Let's conclude with one of my favorite quotes from the great philosopher, author, and speaker Jim Rohn, "The person you become attracts all the things in your life." I live by this quote, and I hope you will too. Be great and go out and create your life full of the success you deserve, as a peak level athlete and human being.

About the Author

Solly Nowrozi is a visionary real estate investor, entrepreneur, former banker, and professional athlete and coach. He is the founder of I&B Investment Co.™ and co-founder of Regal Silk™.

Throughout Solly's squash career, he has been privileged to get coaching and mentorship by some of the greatest squash players, including former world number one and four-time world champion Geoff Hunt; former world number one and world champion Vicki Cardwell; former world number five Dan Jenson; former world number four Stewart

Boswell; former world number one Nicol David; and former world number three and British Open winner Anthony Ricketts and Robyn Prentice. Under their guidance, Solly became a former world number seven squash player in juniors and number one in the Australia and Oceania region. Solly's vision is to add value to his family, investors, team, community, and country through his businesses.

Email: support@ibinvestment.co
Website: www.eregalsilk.com

CHAPTER TWENTY
BREATH, EYES, FOCUS, AND OTHER PEAK PERFORMANCE TOOLS

By Maximus Redfield
Professional Football Player, Model, Actor
Orange County, California

If not now, when? If not me, who?
—Malcolm X

The essence of being a successful athlete is performance. For an athlete to have any kind of success, and especially an elite athlete, you must be able to perform or play to the best of your ability on demand and in the most high-pressure moments. To become an elite athlete, you must have virtually or seemingly complete control over your mind, body, and even your spirit to a certain extent under the most challenging circumstances.

But how do you go about achieving this complete control of your mind, body, and spirit? Is this possible? Can this be learned? Does it include practice and repetition? Yes. Does it include some muscle memory, lots of energy, focus, attention, and intention? Yes. But there are other aspects too, of course. We can define those aspects along with a set of variables all of which when combined within an athlete necessarily produces elite performance or prosperous and abundant outcomes. What are these variables? How do you practice them? How do you know what to practice?

First and foremost, each of us has an inner compass, a forever knowing, a divine connection to our spirit, our soul, our essence, which is also directly and forever connected with God, the Universe, the Divine Source, the Infinite Force, Yahweh, Allah, or however you choose to articulate and perceive this higher, forever power. This sometimes shows itself as "instinct" or "intuition." Through our mindset and mentality, we filter this limitless energy and direct it in the ways that we choose.

As humans, we are habitual creatures, so although we have free will and the power to choose at all times, our habits and subconscious beliefs guide and direct a lot of what we do. Regardless—YOU have the power to take control of this and create habits and beliefs for yourself that are empowering, liberating, and enlightening. Just like anything, step by step, breath by breath is how you start and build momentum until it becomes smooth and natural flowing like a river.

How do you know the correct or best way to train your mind so that in turn your body and spirit is best prepared to perform whatever action is necessary for success and victory? You learn it, of course, and there are many different teachers that you have access to.

Even though our natural ability is very important, our mindset is by far the most important and controllable factor in achieving peak performance and being an elite athlete. Considering this, you must utilize different resources, tools, and tactics to train and develop your mind, just as you train and develop the body and spirit. All three of these things are intimately connected, and this is why you need to dedicate attention and energy to each. All parts—mind, body, and spirit—are guided and directed through the conscious mind-brain complex that thinks and knows its thinking.

Not all thoughts that you experience are "yours." Read that again please. I'll write it again too, just in case—not all thoughts that you experience are "yours."

Whether it is memories and past experiences, best or most traumatic moments, your environment and the people around you, or subconscious beliefs and thought systems—all of these can produce thoughts in your mind even though they aren't relevant to your current environment or situation or you didn't necessarily choose for them to be there or consciously create them yourself. This is why all thoughts are not yours. This is why MOST thoughts are not yours. Being aware of this is a huge advantage as an athlete and absolutely necessary to achieve peak performance.

Without this awareness, you can be thrown off or feel certain emotions and feelings about the wide variety of thoughts that come up that aren't necessarily beneficial or relevant to the current situation. Of course, this amplifies, becoming much more intense during an athletic performance or event, especially when it has large implications. This is why it is even more important for athletes to be aware of this and turn it into an advantage.

What are some ways to overcome such obtrusive thoughts? You and all athletes have many tools that you can utilize, but first let's look at the ultimate tool and solution that is forever available for you—your breath.

The Tool of Your Breath

Have you ever noticed how fast your breath is when your adrenaline is pumping or when you are scared? Have you ever noticed your breath when you are relaxing or feeling focused? How about when someone is yelling at you or you're in a game under pressure?

You might realize that the speed or frequency of your breath, as well as the depth or length of each breath, has a direct influence on your state of mind or the type of thoughts you are experiencing. This is powerful and typically overlooked. In the past few decades or so in Western culture, experts have started to shine a light onto the nature of the breath and all the implications it has on our mind, body, and spirit, and this appreciation will continue. Yoga and meditation have become just as popular in our modern-day Western society as they have always been in Eastern Asian cultures, as well as other places in the world. Both of these practices are centered around the breath and how to utilize it.

In yoga, different poses, stretches, and body positions are practiced and paired with the breath (i.e., consciously breathing and changing the depth and frequency of the breath at different times for different positions) to loosen muscles, stimulate blood flow, and provide other benefits to the body, mind, and spirit. When someone is breathing erratically or inconsistently while doing these various positions, they won't maximize a given pose's full potential. This is true for athletes playing various kinds of sports as well. All sports are based on performance and the ability to execute particular abilities to the fullest in order to be successful.

When an athlete becomes aware of the importance of the breath, they gain a unique skill that can be used in many ways including the following:

- maintaining and enhancing a flow state or zoom focus
- speeding up the body's recovery or lessening the time needed to recover from fatigue,
- stimulating healing from physical ailments
- balancing and stabilizing emotions
- producing more dynamic force (from weightlifting, to football, to ice skating athletes utilizing sharp, intentional breaths before or during a high-force output or intense movement to increase their ability to create force or do a dynamic movement).

Along with these examples, the breath can also be used to ease the mind and release thoughts and emotions that are associated with those thoughts, which aren't beneficial or don't necessarily serve any purpose in that moment or in general.

Using the breath is a game changer, a life changer. In cryotherapy (a two- to five-minute treatment where a person stands in a 360-degree machine from the neck down and receives shots of air that are negative 200 degrees Fahrenheit, more or less), ice tubs, and acupuncture, the breath is tool that is used to maintain mental composure, so the participant can reap the benefits of the healing treatment.

There are multiple other examples of how the breath is utilized as a tool for the mind, body, and spirit. Whether it's Kobe Bryant before a free throw in the NBA finals, Michael Phelps before an Olympic gold medal race, or Roger Federer before a match point serve in a Grand Slam Championship, they all utilize a deep breath or some kind of conscious breath to bring them to the right state of mind to perform to the best of their ability when everything is on the line and it matters most.

Your breath is a tool that is forever available for you, so use it to your advantage. Some athletes use their breath to stir up or conjure emotion within themselves. Whether it is rage, excitement, or gratitude, the breath can be used to immerse yourself further within that feeling. Of course, there is a balance to this and you can utilize the breath as well to maintain within yourself a balance that serves your highest performance and purpose.

The Tool of Emotional Intelligence

Similar to how you can harness your breath and use it as a tool, you can utilize emotional intelligence to serve this same purpose. You can purposefully employ the emotions that act as fuel for you and also determine which ones don't necessarily serve your highest potential in a certain moment, experience, competition, or confrontation.

In my perspective, the phrase "emotional intelligence," refers to your awareness of your feelings when they arise as well as your awareness of where they came from and how to best utilize them for your own highest good and everyone else's. Every successful elite athlete has and utilizes emotional intelligence. Some would go so far as to say they are driven by it and it gives them an edge. Many of those considered the greatest athletes of all time have a deep and powerful passion that at times looks like rage, at times looks like euphoria, and at other times looks like love. When this is out of balance, it can drain a player's performance and can distract and diminish a player's ability to perform.

Although emotional intelligence isn't necessarily a mindset tool, there are techniques that you can use to manage and maximize upon your emotional intelligence. A couple of these techniques include awareness of self-talk and expecting the best outcome. Self-talk refers to the "voice in our head," the "angel and devil on each shoulder," the "inner critic," or whatever else people might call it. Self-talk is a real phenomenon that needs to be learned and mastered because it is absolutely crucial to thriving in any sport, competition, and life in general. During the heat of competition or a seemingly overwhelming moment, it is easy to immediately draw focus to negative plays, mistakes, or outcomes that have happened in the past to us or to others, which we've heard about from family, friends, or acquaintances or that we've seen in a show or movie.

In our society it is popular to criticize and draw intense focus and attention on "bad plays" or "worst-case scenario" outcomes equally to, or if not more than, the amazing plays or "best-case scenario" outcomes. This is because "everybody does it," or "I was just being sarcastic." How many times have you or someone you know joked about something bad happening or was being sarcastic about something bad happening, and then it ended up happening? Yes, we all have the ability to speak life and influence our reality, which intensifies with emotions. Of course, there are other factors that associate these intense emotions with the seemingly undesirable outcomes, but we'll focus on a few. One of these intense emotions, surprisingly, is joy.

Through comedy and socially acceptable norms, we, as humans, often use self-deprecating jokes and terrible hypothetical situations to create a happy or desirable connection or sense of common ground with others. Imagine an elite tennis player carrying a big potted plant down some stairs and joking to their neighbor how it would be terrible if they fell. They might be doing this to create rapport with the neighbor, but in doing so, they are also voicing a negative possibility. Negative thoughts and words can appear during a competition and might even contribute to undesirable outcomes. Although we like to avoid our feelings of fear and shame, we need to be aware of our self-talk and internal programming in order to give the power back to ourselves. By being aware of the voice of the inner critic, we can override those thoughts with empowering ones and reassure ourselves of our success. We can use positive expectations and visualize best-case scenarios to focus our energy and attention on in order to reach that desired reality.

There is an old saying, "Energy flows where attention goes." Therefore, by focusing on and visualizing the best-case scenarios and the most satisfying and fulfilling outcomes, you are drawn closer to that physical reality. You can do this at any time, and the more that you exercise it, then the more noticeable the impact is. In basketball, visualize sending the ball home, expecting every shot to go in. In chess, visualize winning and all the different moves that can contribute to you winning and all the different ways you can achieve victory.

The Tool of Focal Points

In any sport or competition, there are important factors that stand out and demand more attention and development. Master these focal points and you are well on your way to peak performance and being elite in your realm. Focal points are resources that can be used to finetune an athlete's performance. These are incredibly important and are usually the details that separate the elite athletes from just good or average athletes. Regardless of the athlete or sport, focal points are present and an athlete can utilize and integrate them into their knowledge to take their game to a new and higher level.

For example, a focal point of shooting the basketball is eye placement and hand placement. If the positioning of the hands is off or inadequate, then the entire shot is compromised. Similar to this, if the shooter of a basketball doesn't have their eyes on the hoop or focused on a certain part of the rim (some famous or notable shooters have said to have the back of the rim as the focal point of their eyes when they shoot the ball), then there is a significantly lower chance for making the shot. One missed shot when it matters most can lose a championship or be the difference in a player becoming professional and playing for millions of dollars or finishing a career in college and not having that opportunity.

Another example of the importance of focal points and how they are present in all sports can be shown through golf. Although basketball and golf are two very different sports, the same tools and resources can be applied to maximize upon someone's natural ability to be successful and considered elite or one of the best. In golf there are various focal points that directly determine how effective a golfer is. Two of them are hand placement on the golf club (which contributes to the quality of the swing and how effectively the ball is hit) and foot placement or the golfer's stance when hitting the ball.

If a golfer's hand placement is just slightly off or different from what they normally use, then it can cause disaster for where they hit the ball and where the ball lands. Because of the size of the ball and the distance to the hole, the slightest change in form or technique can cause a major change and be disastrous for any golfer, but especially a professional golfer because the margin of error is so small. The placement and positioning of the golfer's feet has this same dramatic effect on changing the trajectory and direction of the ball. The feet are the foundation for the entire swing and body, making those previously stated focal points of hand placement and foot placement/positioning that much more important.

In addition to these focal points that are within ourselves (or seemingly "in our control"), there are also focal points that are outside of us that we need to adapt to and handle accordingly to be successful in our respective sport to achieve peak performance. To explore these focal points, let's continue with the same two example sports of basketball and golf. In basketball, the other players on the court (teammates and opponents) are focal points that have a huge impact on how an athlete plays the game and which strategies are most effective. When a basketball player is aware of the types of teammates that they are playing with and their strengths, it makes them more successful because they can feed and play off of these strengths. In terms of opponents being focal points, this could entail the athlete studying tendencies of opponents in order to diminish opportunities for those opponents to be able to engage their best moves and to discover and exploit their opponents' weaknesses.

This studying, extra information, and a heightened awareness all directly impact and influence the athlete's ability to process information in the most important moments in the competition. Because, let's be honest, that is what all competitions are about, the finish, who wins, and who performed best when it mattered most. This is what all mindset tools are contributing to and feeding into: your ability and speed to process and respond to information. From tracking a 100-mile-an-hour fastball so that it can be hit hundreds of feet, to kicking a soccer ball in the right spot at the right time to go into the goal past the goalkeeper—every sport and situation in life demands the ability to process lots of information in a short amount of time and in turn execute accordingly.

The tools I've outlined in this chapter are available for you to achieve your own peak performance. Nothing can stop you—except you.

About the Author

Maximus Redfield can be considered as many things, a professional athlete, an actor, a model, an author, an entrepreneur. As a University of Notre Dame alumni, former All-American, and International Professional Athlete, Maximus has encountered many profound and powerful experiences in a variety of environments within all walks of life. In reality, none of these things can come close to defining him. His purpose is to be the loving light that the world needs and to utilize all of his abilities, talents, and resources to the fullest so that he leaves a most magnificent mark on the world.

Website: www.maxredfield.com
LinkedIn: https://www.linkedin.com/in/maximus1/

CHAPTER TWENTY-ONE

STEP 2 THE PLATE AND RAISE YOUR GAME

By Shari Reiniger
Performance Consultant, Olympic Baseball Official
Edmonton, Alberta, Canada

My motto was always to keep swinging. Whether I was in a slump or feeling badly or having trouble off the field, the only thing to do was keep swinging.
—Hank Aaron

Like most young athletes, I dreamed of going to the Olympics. I loved watching gymnastics in the summer and ski jumping in the winter. When baseball and softball finally won their place in the Olympics, I was glued to our television set. To watch athletes bring their best performances to the Olympic stage—to see the thrill of victory and the agony of defeat—was always inspiring and humbling.

Becoming an Olympic athlete is such a hard-earned opportunity, and I was nowhere near that level. I didn't realize there was another path to the Olympics, and I never dreamed that was even a possibility. And yet, suddenly I found myself in a group of experienced technical officials and was given the rare opportunity to join the Olympic technical officials team running baseball at the Olympics. Wow, what a moment!

Tokyo 2020 was not a destination I was swinging for. It was simply an incredible stop on my journey. Standing on the field in Fukushima as the ceremonial opening pitch was thrown was a goose-bumps moment I'll never forget. Watching my Japanese friends bring baseball back to the Olympics after a 13-year hiatus was simply amazing.

Suddenly, I thought about all the steps in my journey that led to that day. All of the choices, experiences, and people that took a small-town girl from playing junior college softball in Northern California to coaching baseball in Canada to running the field at the Olympics. How each new opportunity had led me to exactly that place in time. How saying yes made all the difference in the world. Saying yes:

- To play on the varsity high school softball team my freshman year
- To teach high school dance camps across the US during college
- To the love of my life at home plate on the baseball field his father built
- To play university field hockey after becoming a wife and a mom and win a Canadian University Bronze Medal
- To lead the grounds crew at a local baseball complex for the U15 National Championship
- To run a couple of marathons ... that was hard!
- To chair the coaches' selection committee at our local baseball association
- To be the first female head coach of our provincial girls' baseball team
- To be the only female playoff director for our provincial baseball association
- To be the first woman assigned as a technical commissioner at a Baseball World Cup
- To be the only female to sit on our National Baseball Federation's long-term athlete development committee
- To coach at the World Children's Baseball Fair
- To attack "out of my comfort zone" black diamond downhill ski runs
- To be the first woman assigned as an international baseball technical commissioner at the Olympic Games
- To write a chapter in this *Peak Performance: Mindset Tools for Athletes* book ...

It's surreal to realize how random of a chance it is for life to lead to something that seemed to be so out of reach. To be in the right place at the right time doing the right work with the right people surrounding me. Each opportunity always seems to make the next challenge doable. So just say yes!

When I stood on the field in Yokohama after working the gold medal game, I could clearly see four keys to success in my journey that gave me the chance to join the road to Tokyo. Four strategies that I know can help you in your journey as an athlete, as a leader, and in life.

S—Step in the Box and Swing!

The single best piece of advice I can give you as an athlete is to go for it. No baseball player ever hits a World Series-winning home run without stepping in the box and taking a ton of swings. And no junior college softball player gets a chance to run the baseball field for games at the Olympics without stepping to the plate and taking a lifetime of swings along the way.

Before you step in that box, take a look around and understand the game situation. Be clear what your goal is; then do the work needed to prepare. Gather the tools you need, find coaches and mentors to guide you, visualize the pitches you know you'll see, and take some practice swings. Then get your game face on, your mindset right, and step in the box.

No matter what goal you decide to focus on—always go all in. Success never comes to those who only dip their toes in the water. If you want to take your game to the next level, you must commit and find a way to make it happen. Dig into that box and get ready to swing!

Does it sound like I'm talking to a hitter? Yes! Because every time we step in the box in baseball, sport, or life, we need a good approach. Have a plan before you step in, prepare to the best of your ability, then step in with a positive mindset, and be ready to perform. This is your chance to do something big, to learn something new, or to simply support your team and drop down a sacrifice bunt.

Now you're in the box and the pitch is on its way. Are you going to watch three good pitches go by, or are you going to swing? Find the courage to take that first swing and keep swinging. That single moment we finally make solid contact builds amazing self-confidence that is irreplaceable.

When on a trip with my husband years ago, I'll never forget watching how a coach helped someone take her first swing. We signed up for the flying trapeze. Even with the safety harness attached and the net below, it's pretty daunting to step onto that platform, let alone step off of it. A lady in our trapeze group was really scared to go up there but had signed up and decided she was going to do it. What courage! She stood and climbed the ladder. Then, with the safety harness on, she stepped onto that platform, with one hand on the bar and one hand on the support cable.

Ready, hep! It was time to drop off that platform … and she was still standing there.

Ready, hep … still standing there … frozen in fear.

One of the trapeze instructors climbed back down with her and then sat with her on the bench below while the rest of us took our chance to swing. And somehow she found the courage to climb back up the ladder. When she was harnessed up, her coach simply hugged her around the waist while she grabbed the bar with both hands, and he gently dropped her, so she could swing.

Wow!

We were all so proud of this stranger in our group who climbed back in that box and took her chance to swing. She was our inspiration that day and inspires me to this day.

No matter how unsure or scared you might be, find a way to step in the box and take that first swing.

You might struggle to begin with. Remember that swinging and missing is part of the game … and part of life. Baseball Hall of Famers fail seven out of 10 times at the plate. Challenge yourself and push your own boundaries. Just keep stepping in the box to swing until you start making contact then raise your sights as you gain skill and confidence. You never know; one day you just might hit one out of the park.

T—Team Up and Take the Lead

When we include other people as we develop new skills and play the game, we become invested in one another's journeys and success.

True teammates care more and are willing to work harder by each other's sides, so team up with other people as often as you can. Bring people together who share the same passion, goals, and values. Surround yourself with those who are willing to go above and beyond to get the job done. Work with people, and they will work with you. Plus, you might just make a friend or ally for life.

Sometimes teaming up means jumping in to help someone else achieve *their* goals. When you take your eyes off yourself and focus on others, magic often happens. So, when you see a teammate or coach who needs your help, jump in to get the job done.

I couldn't achieve my Olympic dream without many amazing people along the way. I've been surrounded by mentors who supported and pushed me beyond my comfort zone because they believed in me. So always surround yourself with people who challenge and grow you. Find people who believe in you and who cheer you on.

I always say that working in international baseball allows me to see amazing baseball, but it's the people who are always the best part.

Now, what do you do when nobody is stepping up to lead? Why not step in and lead yourself?

Leading does not mean being the boss of others, so simply be the person who brings people together for the next battle on the field, court, or ice. Find ways to remove obstacles and support those who are working hard beside you. No title is needed to lead, you just need to care about the people around you as much as or more than the result.

Some people lead from the front, others from the back, and some right from the middle. Find positive approaches to leading people and they will look for ways to work with you and have your back when the game is on the line. Every team needs multiple leaders so be willing to step up and lead where you're strongest and can make a difference.

E—Evolve and Elevate Your Game

If there's one thing that's guaranteed in this world, it's change. If we're slow to change, the world will pass us by, so open your mind to new possibilities and approaches. This includes finding new ways to train, perform, and bring value as an athlete, teammate, or leader. Remember Einstein's definition of insanity? Sometimes we need to change our approach if we expect to get a different result. So, if your current training program is hindering progress more than it's helping, then ask yourself why and be willing to evolve.

As sport becomes more data driven and visible, we all need to find ways to adapt and adjust to ensure our skills stay relevant. As a technical commissioner, my role started as more of a technical field/rules manager and has evolved to include more of a stage manager role.

Find ways to widen your skill set and add new tools to your toolbox. Even the best baseball pitchers evolve to add new pitches to their arsenal as batters start to find success. Rethink your tried-and-true approaches. There might be new ways to train or *think the game* that didn't exist even two years ago. Find online programs or gurus you can tap into. Find people who are making the impact you are striving for. Keep evolving and keep growing.

The only way to grow to the next level is to stretch your skills and go to the next level. You can certainly create a lot of confidence when you practice and prepare at a level where you are the top performer. But you'll never make the jump to the next level until you experience that next level. You simply must get out of your comfort zone to stretch your skills and learn how to perform at the next level. When you get too comfortable, you're simply not growing. So get uncomfortable.

Each time I'm asked to work at another level, I feel a bit nervous. But here's the thing. I've been nervous before and survived. In fact, sometimes I thrived. I trust my leaders to stretch me enough, so I can grow and still be an asset. That's not to say that I haven't stumbled and had to pick myself back up either. Sometimes we face a challenging situation and get it right ... and sometimes we learn. Simply do your best to learn from your mistakes and add them into your "been there, done that" toolbox.

P—Power Your Game Through Process and Progress

One thing we all see today are people who want to rush the journey and jump straight to the top. I'm the first person to cheer others on when they take their game to the next level. But I also believe it's vital that we *learn, then earn* each step up. Missing steps along the way can come back to haunt you in the end, so don't rush. People who climb Everest train for at least a year and spend a minimum of four weeks making treks up and down the mountain from base camp just to get their body ready for the final climb. Without that process, there's no way they'd be able to summit, let alone survive.

Maybe you've heard the mantra that "slow is fast"? That's been my experience in international baseball. My first Women's Baseball World Cup was in 2004, and I didn't get another assignment until 2008. I worked four Women's World Cups before getting a U15 (Boys) World Cup assignment in 2014. And then my path started speeding up with my first U18 Men's event in 2017 followed by a technical director role in 2018. Then another U18 and my first professional-level event in 2019 just before being assigned to the Olympic qualifier and the Olympic Games.

Sometimes it takes time for new doors to open, no matter who you are or how good you are at your role. Sometimes that big door never opens, and sometimes it opens only for a moment and closes forever. The key is being ready and stepping through that door if it opens.

I'm not always the most patient person, and I tend to dive in head first before looking at what I'm diving into. So, I'm thankful my coaches and leaders gave me a wide range of experiences before offering elevated roles. I'm sure we've all seen what happens when people get thrown into levels they're not ready for. We literally set them up to fail and can lose them in the process.

In baseball, we tell our athletes to trust the process, and I'll say the same thing to you here as well. If you have a trusted coach or mentor helping you lay out a plan, then follow it and evaluate it regularly. Build your patience muscle as you focus on ways to widen and deepen your skill set. Build those bridges to your next level and be ready to cross that bridge when your name is called.

Just. Don't. Give. Up.

The final message I want to give you is that progress is the name of the game. Demanding perfection from yourself means setting yourself up for constant disappointment. Instead, focus on a growth mindset—where you fail forward to learn and grow—and make progress for life.

We took our son to a baseball camp in Phoenix one year, a camp run by a good baseball friend, Orv Franchuk, who at the time was the Boston Red Sox Minor League Hitting Coordinator. He was joined as a camp chair by Joe Maddon, who was then the Angels' bench boss. My husband always talked to our kids about quality at bats, so when Coach Maddon told us how they tracked a quality-at-bat stat the year they won the World Series, we immediately adopted it. We didn't share actual batting stats the entire year. We focused on quality at bats as we competed against older and stronger teams. We noticed that when our team's quality-at-bats stats improved, so did everyone's individual and team performance. Our kids went on to win the U15 Baseball Canada National Championship that year and learned a strong approach for life as 15-year-olds.

When you focus on quality effort and decision-making, it eventually pays off. So ask yourself whether your *process is leading to progress.* That is the magic formula for success, no matter what field you play on.

Bringing It Home

Whenever I talk to athletes about a peak performance mindset, I always focus on how they can STEP to the plate with a champion mindset:

Step in the Box and Swing
Team Up and Take the Lead
Evolve and Elevate
Power Your Game Through Process and Progress

We never truly know where our journey in sport or life will take us, so my question to you is this:

Are you willing to say yes?
I can't wait to see what happens when you do.

About the Author

Shari Reiniger is a performance consultant in Edmonton, Alberta, Canada. She was raised in Northern California by parents who always encouraged her to go for it.

Shari was the first woman assigned as an international baseball technical commissioner at the Tokyo Olympic Games and helped lead the field for the historic opening game and both medal games.

Shari's motto is to "Step 2 the Plate and Raise Your Game." She has lived this motto her entire life and believes everyone can do the same. Whether dancing at the Statue of Liberty Weekend, playing shortstop on her junior college softball team, winning a bronze medal at the Canadian University National Field Hockey Championship, coaching at the World Children's Baseball Fair, or working alongside her international baseball colleagues, Shari keeps stepping to the plate to swing.

Join Shari to inspire the next generation to Step 2 the Plate and Raise Their Game.

Email: shari@step2theplate.com
LinkedIn: https://www.linkedin.com/in/shari-reiniger-645b0815/
Twitter: @fuel2win

CHAPTER TWENTY-TWO
KEYS TO PEAK PERFORMANCE

By Kylie Tullipan
Owner, CoachedByKylie, Strength & Movement Expert
Marina del Rey, California

Reaching peak performance is not a sometime thing. There is not a peak performance switch you can turn on in competitions. Peak performance is a mindset that guides an athlete's choices, decisions, and actions every day.
—Ken Ravizza, sport psychologist

On February 22, 2014, I was crushed and excited at the same time. After almost a year of training, I heard the words no one wants to hear, "You failed." That was fail number one. I went back to the drawing board, back to training, rep after rep, trying to build my strength and get out of my head, with the goal of nailing the five reps with a pair of 16-kilogram bells required for my StrongFirst Level 1 certification.

Fast forward to June 26, 2014. I walked into DogTown CrossFit, just as the 4 p.m. class started. Music was pumping, Adam was coaching class, and Kettlebell, his dog, greeted me with a big hug and lick on the face. This day was going to be special because the times before when Kettlebell greeted me, I PR'd (set a personal record). She was my lucky charm.

Adam asked what I was doing all dressed up and so late since I usually trained early in the morning. I had hurried in from a meeting. I changed into my ever-faithful black tights and DT tank-top and took to my back corner of the gym. Today was the day I had to get the press if I was to avoid re-sitting the full certification. The pressure was on. I did my normal warm-up routine, got to my press, and followed my program to the last details. I decided to go for it, so I set up my video.

Rep 1 went up, reps 2 and 3 went up, and now when I started to doubt myself, I got in my head and told myself, "No doubting!" Rep 4 went up. I was getting so excited, trying to stay focused and putting that energy into my last rep. Rep 5 went up, and I screamed with excitement, "F---yeah!" I slammed the bells down.

Everyone in the gym wondered what had happened. I ran over to Adam, showed him the videos, and said, "See, I got it."

That's when he said the words no one wants to hear. "You failed."

What had happened was that in doing that final rep, I'd lost focus, let my emotions take control, and instead of finishing the final rep cleanly, I'd returned the bells unsafely. All that work had gone to waste.

As a result of that experience and the trials and successes reaching my goals over the years following that failure, I honed in on some of the most important key ingredients to having a peak performance mindset. I look forward to sharing these with you now

Just like, a high-performance driver must become one with the car, a comedian one with their audience, and a rower one with their oar and crew, we must become one with ourselves, our goals, our values, our purpose, our body, and our mind. To achieve peak performance, we must think, feel, and move like champions in all areas of our life. So, how do we do it?

Concentration and mental toughness are the margins of victory.
—Lewis Hamilton, Seven times Formula 1 Champion.

The difference between a player and a champion is that a champion doesn't rely on intuition and talent alone. We only need to look at athletes like Michael Phelps, who has the wingspan of a Boeing 747, and Roger Federer, who has the timing and accuracy of a Swiss watch, to see talent and physical ability isn't all it takes.

Champions like these might have some great natural abilities, but they are heavily invested; they use strong tactics and strategies, take ownership and responsibility, and train themselves and their craft's physical, mental, and emotional side. How else do they handle the pressure of game day or the highs and lows of their career?

We can all learn to think like champions, but will we be champions in every moment? Life and sport are a dynamic with many pieces, ever-changing and always moving. Your physical abilities are quite steady and consistent in contrast to your mental abilities; your mind flutters from moment to moment due to pressures to perform, situational environmental demands, distractions, stress, etc., but some key tools can help you train your mental dexterity.

You can see how I became so overwhelmed and excited to finally press that fifth rep, that I lost focus and failed the rep because I didn't return the bells safely. Your emotions and mind chatter can take your focus, overwhelm you, and cost you the results you desire. Hard work doesn't always pay off, but your ability to sustain focus under pressure definitely does. The difference between performance and peak performance is your mind.

Performance Domains

Your Performance has three domains:

1. Technical—your ability to do a specific sport, i.e., row a boat, race a car, etc.
2. Physical—movement, mobility, endurance, speed, power, etc.
3. Mental—this holds it all together; it includes your beliefs, purpose, and mindset.

Being strong and capable in just one domain is not good enough. It is important to train in all three—technical, physical, mental—if you are to perform at your best. You can see this from my example at the start of the chapter. During my first press test, I had the technical ability, but I didn't have the strength needed for the necessary five reps. Then, during my second attempt, I possessed both the technical and the physical requirement, but my mental ability—my mindset—to maintain focus was my missing link.

But what is mindset? Mindset refers to how you think, feel, and perceive yourself and the world around you. Mindset significantly impacts how you act and perform in the context of both life and sport—a positive attitude, acceptance of constructive criticism, and attention to detail go a long way in the world of high performance.

We often think that performance is the end result. However, no matter how well you prepare, train, and take care of things within your control, your mindset ultimately leads to performance anxiety if you're fixated on the end result. Why? The short answer is your focus. The final result is a combination of taking care of things within your control (training, sleep, etc.) plus the things outside of your control (teammates, weather, etc.) Peak performance is the ability to navigate these things and focus on the right thing at the right time, not simply the end result, winning the race, lifting a PR.

See, focusing on the result is what you call a finite game. You see everything in a fixed way, as win or lose, black or white. You are focusing on the future, which is yet to happen, and you are attaching an expectation of feeling x or receiving y, attaching your happiness onto something that is not fully in your control, instead of focusing on the moment you are in and aligning it with your core values and purpose being as one with you, your goal, and that moment in time.

Think about what would happen if you are in the final few meters of a race about to cross the finish line in first place, or you are swinging over half your bodyweight with a kettlebell, and for a moment, you shift your focus to the competitor next to you or the voice in your head saying you can't do this? Or what if you are diving off a cliff 50 feet tall, or driving a race car and taking a corner at 190 miles per hour, and for a split second, you shift your focus from the task at hand to that time in practice you fell or crashed or to the beat of your racing heart? You'd most likely lose the race, drop the bell, or worse. It is vital to focus on the here and now, and catch yourself listening to the tiny voice in your head and changing it if needed.

The opposite to all of this and key in having a peak performance mindset is to have a growth mindset; Play the infinite game and know you have done all you can for what is in your control and be as well prepared so that what is not in your control has minimal impact.

You could say that peak performance is the art of repeated deliberate practice. It is not about succeeding all the time or even being happy all the time. It is about your ability to adjust and pivot to maintain the highest level of focus in any one moment without distraction.

Mindset

There is more to mindset than just positive thinking and visualization. Mindset consists of:

- Communication with self, and others, teammates, coaches, etc.
- Concentration on what is important now
- Control with technical (strength and conditioning) training and knowing the rules or standards
- Physiology regarding posture, breathing, movement, and mechanics, and letting your interests, values, and goals motivate you
- Commitment to valuing yourself, as well as your commitment to identify how to improve and incrementally improve

You can see from the above elements that a lot of performance is behavioral, and behaviors can be learned and trained. You can say that the physical aspect of your training and the data is the science, and the mental and behavioral aspect is the art. Furthermore, we can look at this as a pyramid with communication, concentration, control, and physiology all building on each other, leading up towards the pinnacle of commitment.

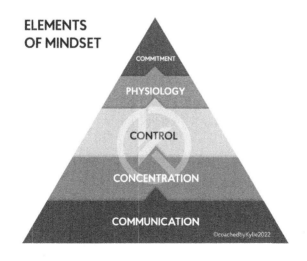

Purpose Is the First Step to Winning

Champions aren't made in the gyms. Champions are made from
something they have deep inside them—a desire, a dream, a vision.
—Muhammad Ali

As we know, focus alone will not get you started, nor will it sustain you during the crazy, exciting, and sometimes turbulent roller-coaster ride you take on when pursuing your goals, sporting or other. Purpose, on the other hand, will help.

The difference between purpose and a goal is that your goal is something you wish to achieve, and purpose is the reason, and it relates to your core values. To help in understanding yourself, why you do things, and why you want to achieve things, you need to understand your core values.

Define Your Core Values

Your core values play a major part of the psychological element of mindset. They are important because these become your litmus test, your compass for your key decisions. When you are faced with going out and partying, or staying and training, ask yourself, "Does this serve my values, my purpose, and my goals?"

Your mindset is the way you think. It's an "established set of attitudes," a collection of thoughts and beliefs that shape your mental habits. These thought patterns impact what you think, feel, and do, how you see the world, and how you make sense of yourself. Simply put, your core values shape your mindset.

Firmly established core values also help you in tough times so that you become your own cheerleader and don't need external gratification or recognition that is not in your control. You become one with your vision and self.

What are core values?

Values act as guiding principles for how you desire and aspire to behave. For example, as a coach, three of my core values are to educate, empower, and challenge my students.

What are your core values? Try to think of the things that are most important to you, and narrow your list down to your core three. As the name suggests, these values are core to your being. They resonate and speak to you because of something deep inside you based on your experiences and unique worldview. These values are naturally a part of who you are and how you behave when you are at your best and in alignment with your purpose. These values should transcend all contexts of your life. These values are central, distinctive, and enduring about you.

Define Your Goal

Goals are good for setting direction and aid in focus. Even still, every Olympian wants to win gold, yet not all achieve it. That's why core values are important. They give the process a greater meaning and value and bring it back to self.

First, you need to identify the desired goal and vividly imagine it. For example, what does it look like? How do you feel? Who is with you? What's the weather like? What are you seeing, smelling, tasting, and hearing? This detailed imagining will also help you program your subconscious so that the negative voices get fainter and your dreams become you.

Think about a baby learning. As children, we explore or play to learn. And we learn most by engaging *all of our senses*. Our brain develops most in the early stages of crawling because this is when the majority of our senses are being stimulated at once—our sense of touch, sight, hearing, and possibly even taste (if you find something intriguing on the floor). We are motivated to move because we see an object we want to know about. As we begin to walk, fewer of our senses are engaged because we are taking up less surface space and our line of sight is now much higher and further away. Hence, further distraction.

This is why I also chose the word "imagery" and not "visualization," as visualization refers more to the mind's eye. With peak performance, we need to be fully immersed in all our senses to achieve the highest level of focus and the strongest mind to resist distraction (and, in my case, to help me stay calm and not get overwhelmed).

Set a SMART goal. Be specific (S); make it measurable (M), achievable (A), realistic (R), and time-restricted (T). Then you need to attach this to your core values, be it integrity, education, respect, loyalty, challenge, etc.

Train Focus—Practice

Once you know what you want and why you need to train your focus and your inner voice, do the following. First you need to assess what is in your control and not in your control, and seek constructive feedback to minimize distraction, manage expectations, see areas of improvement, etc. This is also part of the art of deliberate practice.

Deliberate practice is a specific kind of practice that is purposeful and structured with the aim to evolve and improve. It requires sharp focus, and the tighter the feedback loop, the better. Each deliberate practice drill should ideally have a clear goal and way to get immediate feedback from students or video playback. This kind of practice gives you small wins on the journey to your goal, which over time helps to build your self-confidence and belief. I record and journal every set in every training session or have a coach with me, giving me feedback in real time. I take notes after each set on each rep. If I try a new cue, set-up, breathing technique, etc., I make a note of it and whether it was successful or not in correcting the intended concern. The devil is in the detail when you are on the path to performing at your best.

Morning and night routines train your subconscious mind, get you "focused" on your day, and focus you on your dreams. These times are ideal for constantly reminding your inner voice of your goals, who you are, and who you are becoming.

Journaling is another great tool to train your focus. You can use general daily and training journals as an accountability tool. Ask yourself in the morning journaling time, "Journal, How will I be a champion today?" And in the evening, "How was I champion today?"

You can train your focus in the gym via the ABC (agility, balance, coordination) intentional deliberate interval training and training distraction, to name two options. Other ways to enhance your focus are via music, puzzles, breathing, and meditation. Your brain is like a muscle; it needs to work and works in conjunction with other parts of your body, so physical training like this helps to improve the brain's cognitive abilities and processing capacity.

We have all heard of flow or being in the zone. You know that transcendent state that is elusive and only happens when you become one with your mind, body, and craft. When it's go time and everything falls into place. When you may feel like you're in a time warp where you're so absorbed in what you're doing that you know you're on track to achieving what you came to do. The flow state can feel like déjà vu.

People with a growth mindset, who play the infinite game, who focus on the right thing at the right time, tend to find flow more easily than others. They also are self-aware, and they self-reflect and self-regulate. They are aware and mindful of their thoughts, actions, and emotions, they set their goals and align them with their purpose, and they create a plan of what needs to be done and understand the parts that are in their control and not. They visualize their ideal self and results daily. They feel everything—the sweat, their heart racing, their butt going numb on the seat, the air blowing. They hear all the noises, taste the air and sweat on their bodies, and know what part of their body is moving when and where. They reflect daily using a journal and keep a daily or pre-game routine to promote focus and calm their nerves. People with a growth mindset seek constructive feedback—this usually means hearing things they don't want to hear, but they will also hear more ways to improve.

Focus is the expression of peak performance, and to help maintain focus and stay on course to achieving your goals, you should understand yourself, your core values, and purpose, as it serves as your compass and keeps you going when things get tough.

The three keys to achieving your optimal self and a peak performance mindset are to use purpose to motivate yourself, practice deliberately and finetune your craft, and focus on the right things in any given moment. Your reward for this is the ability to enter "the zone" or flow state where you can perform effortlessly at peak states.

It wasn't from regular success after success that forged my greatest accomplishments; but rather having a goal and being smart as I worked towards the goal allowed me to find my highest levels of peak performance. Remember, if you can spot greatness in someone else, then you can find it in yourself because only people with similar traits can see those traits in others. So, get started. Define your purpose and set your goal, create your plan, and train while journaling your progress, so you can see your results and remain motivated in a cycle of ever-increasing levels of performance. And remember, a goal without a purpose is a goal without meaning. Your goal is a maker of your greater purpose in athletics and in life.

About the Author

As a former dancer, figure skater, and Ironman triathlete, Kylie Tullipan understands first-hand the importance of a healthy mind-body connection and performance. She has worked in high-stress, high-performance corporate and events management environments, where success is measured by deadlines. Today, she is a seasoned performance coach and certified StrongFirst and CrossFit instructor, as well as a qualified Neuromotive coach with multiple degrees in sports marketing, languages, events, and business. Kylie specializes in kettlebell training that accelerates mindset strength performance.

Performance through excellence remains Kylie's passion, across the intersection of sport and corporate life. Her mission is to bridge the gap between being a competitor and becoming a champion. Performance excellence lives at the intersection of art and science, and Kylie strives to educate, empower, and challenge team members, physically and mentally, to achieve their true potential.

Since moving to the United States from Australia, Kylie has worked with scores of institutions including the California Yacht Club Rowing Team, Marina Aquatic Center, Da Vinci School of Science, and various fitness gyms in workshops and group and individual coaching sessions.

Email: kylie@coachedbykylie.com
Website: www.coachedByKylie.com

CHAPTER TWENTY-THREE
BETTER TODAY THAN YESTERDAY

By Julia Catherine Vincent
2x Olympic Athlete in Diving
Lexington, Kentucky

How do you stay motivated all the time?

Throughout my career, this might be the question I have been asked most, and although I believe it is driven mostly from a curiosity standpoint, I also believe that there is often a reason behind the curiosity. One person's ability to stay motivated over an extended period of time can look very different from another's. I have had many a conversation with people who do struggle with motivation about the ways in which they can overcome such an obstacle because motivation, along with discipline, is an important part of any success story.

There are different forms of motivation and while I do not intend to go into the specifics of these different forms, I do think it is important that I at least touch on the topic of intrinsic versus extrinsic motivation. According to the Merriam-Webster dictionary, for something to be "intrinsic," it must "belong to the essential nature or constitution of a thing." In other words, it must be inherently or innately part of something or someone. Conversely, according to dictionary.com, something that is "extrinsic" is "not essential or inherent, not a basic part or quality, or an outward or external influence."

Intrinsic motivation is driven by your own desire to achieve more without external factors such as rewards, etc., playing a part in that desire. Although not all people are programmed in the same way and staying motivated might be more difficult for some than others, I believe drawing motivation from an internal place rather than an external place is an essential practice in order to sustain motivation over a long period of time.

Let me give you an example. Imagine you are a high-performing athlete competing at the Olympic games and you achieve your life-long dream of medaling. This ranks you in the top three in the world, and you stand on the podium as happy as can be, but once you step off, you think to yourself, "I really thought that would feel more satisfying than it did." Unfortunately, this is the reality for a lot of people after having achieved a dream they have been chasing for years. I am not saying that you should not have big dreams or that you should not chase the goals you have set out for yourself. I whole-heartedly believe that you should chase those dreams and, furthermore, be ready to chase those dreams every single day. What I am saying, though, is that where you place value and importance matters. If the only thing that matters to you is the medal, and you happen to not perform the way that you hoped you would, rebounding after such a knock can be difficult. Even more so, when you do achieve that dream and have a medal-winning performance, where do you go from there if the medal was all that you felt was important, especially if it left you feeling unsatisfied? The test now is being able to draw motivation from somewhere other than that extrinsic desire of achieving the medal because that box has already been checked.

Let's think about another example, imagine you are an athlete with an intense rivalry with one of your competitors, and the only thing that keeps you going at practice is thinking about this competitor and what they're doing to be better. Imagine that the only thought that motivates you is knowing you will have to compete against this rival at your next matchup, but unexpectedly, your rival becomes injured and will not be competing for the next year. Where does this leave you? Where do you draw motivation from when the one thing that motivated you has disappeared? Don't let my words be misconstrued. This form of external motivation can be helpful at times but acknowledging a healthy balance between the two forms is everything. Too much emphasis on an external source of motivation can be detrimental if there is not enough emphasis on internal motivation.

Allow me to elaborate on one of my own personal experiences that forced me to look inward for motivation rather than relying on external sources. I was an NCAA Division 1 student-athlete for the University of South Carolina, graduating in 2018 (for any Gamecocks out there, #gococks). Once my collegiate career came to an end, I decided to continue training at the University of South Carolina and pursue my professional career, diving for my home country of South Africa. The decision to continue my career with my college coach, Todd Sherritt, was the greatest decision for me, and we went on an incredible journey of highs and lows. At times, however, training with a coach that was responsible for the college team meant that when the team was traveling for collegiate competitions, I was training completely on my own. Now, I don't mean, on my own with no teammates. I mean, completely on my own without my coach or anyone at all that remotely knew anything about diving. I was usually fortunate enough to have a swim coach or lifeguard around for safety reasons during these times, but outside of the safety aspect of their presence on the pool deck, I was being held accountable by no one but myself.

Let me tell you, this forces a different level of independence and self-motivation for an athlete. There is no one there to say, "That wasn't good enough, restart the set," or "Raise the standard, Jules, raise the standard." There's no one to make sure that you're stretching, warming up, or even making sure that you complete the practice in its entirety. Essentially, I could very well have skipped the practice with no one noticing and gone on with my day. These were the days when having the ability to find intrinsic motivation really came to be useful.

It was all-important that on those days, when I woke up knowing that not one person would be at the pool to aid in my motivation or push me to be better, I had to ask myself a few questions before I even got to the pool: "How good do I want to be?", "How can I show up and be just a little better than yesterday?", and "Am I doing everything I can to get myself there?" If I decided not to show up at practice, I definitely was not doing everything that I could. Even if I did show up at practice but only went through the motions, not really giving it my all, I was still not doing everything I could. I had to make sure that when I went in for that day of practice, regardless of who was or wasn't around me, I was doing everything I could to be a better athlete that day than I was the previous day.

These lonely practice days, that often turned into weeks, forced self-reflection and exposed any lack in motivation that I was experiencing.

When there was no one around to impress and no one around to keep me accountable, I was left with the reality of the nature of my true ambitions. Why was I really doing this sport? There was a realization that if I was not going into practice every day with the intention of making myself a better athlete with or without external motivators, I was going to have a hard time with maintaining motivation throughout the entirety of my career.

I can only speak to my own experience in the sport of diving, but going from a college athlete to a professional athlete meant that I was now sometimes without a coach and often without a weekly competition or a weekly analysis to determine my progress. In the world of collegiate sports, competing was a very regular practice all throughout the year, which could change as you entered the professional world of sports. Becoming a professional athlete meant that you were putting in hours of practice every day all year round for one or two competitions for an entire year. If your motivation was solely based on your competitors and the accolades that came along with performing, can you imagine how maintaining motivation would be difficult when these things almost completely diminished from your routine?

Again, I don't want to be misunderstood. Having competitors, teammates, and coaches are all vital parts of being motivated as an athlete, but for a more sustained motivation, I truly believe it has to come from a different place. An internal place that is unwavering and unchanging because there are many external factors over which you may not have control and when these things change, it is easy to feel thrown for a loop.

Is it easy for me to look back now as if it wasn't difficult in the moment? Absolutely. Hindsight is almost always 20/20, remember? There is usually a lot more clarity when you have the opportunity to look back on an experience. What is not always easy, however, is to have the right perspective in the thick of what you are going through at the time. One thing I would say that I've realized over the years is that the accomplishment of representing your country at the Olympic games is a lot less about being in the Olympics itself with all of the lights and eyes on you, and so much more about the journey you go on to get there, as clichéd as that might be. The journey comes down to who you become through all of it and how you are able to be in your own corner every day. To be "in your own corner" will look different for different people, but I believe an imperative part of that is respecting yourself and your journey enough to hold yourself accountable every day and find motivation in the things over which you have control.

Alrighty then, you've been patient enough. It is time to get to some of the good news now! There is reason to have hope when your only goal walking into practice on a given day is to be just a little bit better than you were the day before. That's because it does two important things. It has the potential to take away the pressure of performing at future competitions if you let it, and it aids in taking away the pain or disappointment you might feel from any past failures you've experienced. As a result, it allows you to be fully present, focusing on the task at hand by placing more importance on the process rather than the outcome. This mindset shift is a major part of respecting the journey as a whole.

I'll leave you with one last thought. I imagine a lot of people would rather I pretended that we did not enter a time warp of isolation and heartache two years ago when the global pandemic, COVID-19, rolled through our world like a giant storm, but unfortunately, it is a great example of a time when intrinsic motivation was crucial to anyone that wanted to continue progressing in their life. Isolation can be a motivation sapper for human beings, especially for the people that are reliant on the energy of others to remain motivated. I felt tested during this time, and I know a lot of other people did too for many reasons. It is during a time like that when the true colors of a person can often be shown, and the truth of those colors is not always too comforting. This truth, about whether your default is to be intrinsically or extrinsically motivated, has the potential to feel disheartening if you fall on the unfavorable side of it, but it does not have to be something that is negative if you're able to recognize the situation for what it is and learn from it. At first, there might be some resistance to changing that outlook, and I wouldn't say it is the easiest of mindsets to change, but I do know that it is worth it.

As an athlete who used to be highly extrinsically motivated and driven by all of the wrong things, I can tell you that I am happier now than I ever have been because I work every day to keep my focus in the right place and keep my desires as intrinsic as I can. I have a changed perspective on the pool deck during practices and a renewed love for the sport. I enjoy even the toughest of practices because I have one focus, and that is to be better that day than the day before. The beauty of being intrinsically motivated is that I am not consumed by external stressors such as an upcoming competition; however, I am able to use the upcoming competition as a way to bring a greater level of intensity to a practice, only if I need to. I have the best of both worlds being able to control exactly how much focus I give the upcoming competition during my practices, ensuring that I only give it enough focus to where it will help my training, not hinder it. There is truly so much freedom in that control alone.

My challenge to you is to take a deep dive into the core of what motivates you. Once you find that out, you have the potential to change your reality as you know it. Put yourself first by showing up, ready and willing to learn. Show up with the mindset to be just a little better than you were yesterday because who knows where that might lead you? Who knows what kind of athlete, leader, competitor, or, more importantly, person you can become?

About the Author

Julia Catherine Vincent is a two-time Olympic springboard diver for her home country of South Africa, competing at the 2016 and 2020 Olympic games. Julia began her career at the age of 14 years old in South Africa before moving to the United States to attend the University of South Carolina in 2014, representing USC for four years at the collegiate level, which is where her career took off. Julia became a Southeastern Conference (SEC) champion, and a National Championship (NCAA) silver and bronze medalist during her time competing for the USC Gamecocks. She has since continued her career professionally where she has become a FINA World Finalist and Semi-Finalist on multiple occasions, and is currently in pursuit of a third Olympic Games in Paris 2024.

Email: julesvincent10@outlook.com
LinkedIn: https://www.linkedin.com/in/julia-vincent-9a536b214/

CHAPTER TWENTY-FOUR
FRAME YOUR PERSPECTIVE

By Adam Whisler, MS, CSCS, CISSN
Tactical S&C Coach, Combat Veteran, Hybrid Athlete
Colorado Springs, Colorado

Life is very short and anxious for those who forget the past, neglect the present, and fear the future.
—Seneca

Remember Your Past

"Alright, Hollie. Throw the paper to that one," I say as we cruise down the neighborhood roads to finish up our daily afternoon paper route.

I turn to check her work throwing the paper when, all of a sudden, she collapses.

"Hollie!" I scream as I jump off my bike and sprint to her side.

Nothing. She can't hear me. She's having another seizure. Not just any seizure, a grand mal seizure. The worst kind.

I'm only 10 years old, but I do as I was instructed by my parents. Turn her on her side. Don't let her choke on her tongue. Push her adult tricycle away to remove objects from the area. Be aware not to get hit myself if her limbs flail. Find help immediately.

Luckily, a neighbor drives past.

I wave and yell at them. "Please! Go down the road to the cul de sac to 5120 and get my parents, now!"

This is my first time being alone with Hollie while she has a seizure. I am beyond scared, but I know what to do because my parents taught me well. My oldest sibling and only sister, Hollie, has a rare inborn metabolic condition called argininosuccinic aciduria (ASA). This impacts her speech development, physical abilities, dietary intake, cognitive functioning, and more.

Despite the odds stacked against Hollie, our mom has been the human version of a saint with her care. Like one of God's angels, our mom is the epitome of hard work, dedication, consistency, patience, kindness, and, of course, perspective.

Without missing a beat, my mom is routinely awake before 5 a.m. to get her daily runs in. She has completed over 60 full marathons in my lifetime, and she's currently on a daily run streak of over 3 years! But my mom is not special because of her ability to run long distances. She is special because she knows the importance of perspective. My mom understands what it means to push your mental and physical limits to their threshold, and she has never let anyone in my family believe we couldn't do something we put our minds to, Hollie included.

In the past two years, Hollie has completed two 5-kilometer walks, one 4-mile walk, and even an entire half-marathon-distance bike ride! She's a Special Olympics bowling state champion and still actively competes in track, swimming, bowling, and the softball toss.

Growing up as Hollie's youngest brother provided me with an amount of responsibility, empathy, and perspective on life that has been invaluable to my success. With every activity I pursue, I know that I need to be grateful for the opportunity to participate at all. To allow myself to give anything less than my best would be an active sacrifice of God's greatest gift, life itself.

No matter what challenges I have faced in life, framing them with my past has been a critical component of my success.

If you are reading this chapter, it is clear to me that you are seeking your own version of peak performance in athletics and in life. One idea that I know to be true is that everyone is going into, going through, or coming out of some challenge. Challenge is one of life's guarantees. While there are clearly levels to the amount of difficulty present in someone's life, there is no escaping adversity in some form.

Leveraging these past experiences can dramatically help you push through new challenges on your way to peak performance. When adversity is staring you down—because you will be faced with adversity along the way—reflect back on prior triumphs. Use the strength you have gained throughout your life to help you face whatever you are facing at the moment. Don't forget the past; use it to your advantage!

As I learned on that street corner at 10 years old, staying in the present moment and reacting to a situation as you are trained can sometimes be the difference between life and death.

Live in the Present Moment

Killing time, one of the guys from my platoon was joking around with word games. "Sir, would you rather throw in a double-decker dip of Copenhagen or …"

Suddenly—*pop, pop, pop.* Bullets fire into the side of the Hesco barriers to our right.

"Contact!" I hear yelled across the base. I immediately go into action, responding to the situation. Just as we had before, we were taking direct fire from the city a couple hundred meters away from tower 5. I sprinted from tower 3 to tower 5 and yelled up to my squad leader, "What's the situation?"

"We're taking direct fire from an AK and PKM about 400 meters away at our 2 o'clock," he says.

"Roger," I say as I key up my radio to alert the tactical operations center (TOC) about the situation.

At this point, we understand our surroundings, know what we are facing, and know the procedures to take care of this engagement. I complete the plan that I created to react to this type of contact from this location, and my platoon responds without fail. They're a fantastic group of soldiers I am lucky to lead.

For the rest of the engagement, the soldiers in my unit do everything they need to defeat the enemy. As the platoon leader, I am constantly communicating with the TOC, the other positions, and my platoon members to stay aware of what needs to be done. By the end of the fight, we are successful and have no casualties. We head into another night of overwatch.

In this circumstance, being fully present in the situation at the moment is vital. While prior training and rehearsals provide the skills, various challenges require your full attention. Training to the point where critical tasks become autonomous is the goal so that you can maximize your attention in the present moment.

Planning for the future is also essential, yet diverting attention to thoughts outside of the situation is useless. Focus on what needs to happen now to maximize your chances for success. Keep the scope of your attention to a brief timeframe that enables your brain to develop solutions to the task at hand.

Many people frequently address the importance of staying in the present moment with various mantras. "Be here, now." "Maximize your minutes." "Seize the day." This is a popular, effective mindset tip for people across all walks of life. The mantra I created and use most for sports performance is, "Convince yourself it's not that bad."

This mantra has been critical in framing my perspective on challenges throughout my personal life and military career. Being an infantryman meant doing hard things ... frequently. Ruck march marathons, jumping out of perfectly good airplanes, Ranger school, and sleeping wherever and whenever possible are just a few of the expectations of being in the infantry.

To thrive in these situations, there needs to be a willingness to enter into the darkness affectionately referred to as the "pain cave." This expression embodies the understanding that the mind enters into a place where it can determine your willingness to continue. Do you suffer through the pain? Is the risk worth the reward? How bad do you want it?

If you want it bad enough, you'll need to face the pain head-on, convince yourself it's not that bad, and endure. What could this venture into the pain cave be preparing you for?

Don't Fear the Future. Prepare for It

Twenty miles into my 31-mile training run, I walk into my small apartment in Fort Drum, New York, to fill up water and quickly grab my gloves, a baseball hat, and glasses before continuing for the next two hours of running. The inclement weather had already started, and I would need the extra gear to finish this training run in the middle of the ice storm rolling in.

The middle of April in Upstate New York can be quite ... frigid. Especially as someone who is not a fan of the cold, I had a hard time training for my next ultramarathon when nearly every training run was a decision between the treadmill or frozen eyelashes.

There are times when reflecting on past accomplishments and drawing mental strength from your history can improve resilience, performance, and attitude. There are also times when staying in the present moment, fully immersed in the immediate tasks at hand is the most appropriate mindset for peak performance. However, there are times when you're required to channel thoughts toward the goals you are seeking to accomplish.

This training run was one of those times. I was three weeks away from my first 50-mile ultramarathon, and this was my peak distance training run in my program. I had to finish. Three weeks from now, no matter what the weather was going to be, I would be pushing through toward the finish line. If I wouldn't let the weather stop me on race day, why would I let the weather stop me on a solo training run? It was time to enter the pain cave and start exploring.

To achieve peak performance in sport and life, it is essential to establish goals for yourself. Whether these goals are short-term, long-term, or process goals, their importance is critical. Goals provide a guidebook for the future because they enable the backwards planning process. This process can be explained as follows.

1. Identify the specific achievements, tasks, or benchmarks that must be completed closest to that end goal.
2. Place them on a reasonable timeline next to the goal itself.
3. Place each additional task, in successive backward order, on a timeline back to the present moment.

For example, I actively compete in ultramarathons and powerlifting. Two conflicting ends of the spectrum, I know. But I love the challenge and polar opposite mental and physical demands that accompany each sport. In power-lifting, the goal is to lift as much weight as possible in the squat, bench, and deadlift for one repetition each. Knowing this, I can take the date of the meet and backwards plan so that I am prepared both physically and mentally to handle the maximal loads I will attempt at the meet.

Each training session throughout the planned program, I know that I am inching closer and closer to the goal of lifting a new personal record. Each time I have the opportunity to build my strength physically, but it is just as challenging mentally. It is not always easy to get under hundreds of pounds on a squat or to deadlift well above twice your bodyweight off the floor. In each instance, I am deep in thought about these challenges prior to the lift.

Perspective about the future goal in mind is an invaluable mindset tool that can be leveraged to maximize the probability of success. When I stare down a heavy barbell or prepare for a long training run, I focus my mindset on the future goals I have in place. The key to applying perspective, in all its forms as a skill, is to practice.

> *Don't explain your philosophy. Embody it.*
> —Epictetus

We can all recall a time when we have seen someone lose their temper, escape any form of emotional control, and struggle to see any bigger picture outside of the current situation. Road rage, getting stuck in heavy traffic, stubbing a toe, or spilling all over the floor. With these images in mind, maybe it feels like something you have experienced at times in your life as well. Gosh, we all have at some point, right?

Yet, this person is not who anyone strives to be. A peak performance mindset is certainly not defined by a lack of social and emotional intelligence. The importance of practicing a peak performance mindset in daily life is critical.

As one of my role models, Ben Bergeron, describes in his coaching practice, the secret to building a better athlete is to start by building better people. Build excellent character traits first, then focus on developing athletic abilities. In sport, daily life, and personal relationships, no one wants to be involved with an individual who is overly emotional, loses their temper, or complains about any and every situation. People do want to be involved with others who are kind, patient, confident, and cooperative.

Placing challenges into perspective is not simply executed while participating in your sport of choice. You cannot become the person you want to be on the playing field without being committed to becoming that person in your daily interactions. Practicing mindfulness, perspective, patience, and the many other mindset tips detailed in this book must be done daily. In the smallest of situations, how do you react?

The next time you are stuck in traffic, burn yourself on the stove, or spill all over the floor, be mindful of your thoughts. Do not allow yourself to practice bad habits. Do not be reactive to the situation. Recall the type of person you want to be when faced with adversity. Actively think about the perspective of the situation. Is it really worth losing emotional control over?

Your mindset is not exclusive to sports. Shaping the person you want to become both on and off the competition floor is the way to make positive changes. Who do you want to be when faced with adversity in any environment?

Instead of explaining your desired philosophies to your friends, family, and teammates, embody them. Embody them to the fullest extent in all areas of life. Be the type of person you want to be each day. Be the type of person that you would like to be around. Build truly excellent character traits, then focus on building athletic abilities.

Throughout my life, I have been given the opportunity to practice perspective as a character trait on a daily basis. I am blessed to have the ability to speak, to run, to jump, to throw, to catch, to learn, to plan, to pray, to follow, and to lead.

Regardless of the adversities I am faced with, I implement the daily practice of perspective. Remembering previous challenging moments in my life helps to reframe my perspective. Being fully present in a daunting task but knowing I have the skills and abilities to succeed helps to reframe my perspective. Focusing on the process of preparing for future critical moments and backwards planning for my biggest goals helps to reframe my perspective.

I am the type of person who lives by core values. I am the type of person who acknowledges the blessings in daily life. I am the type of person who perseveres in the most challenging moments. I am the type of person whom I would want to be around.

What type of person are you?

More importantly, what type of person do you want to become?

About the Author

Adam Whisler is a tactical strength and conditioning coach, PhD student in human performance, army combat veteran, ultra-marathon runner, and powerlifter.

Adam enlisted in the army infantry at 17 years old, commissioned as an officer at 22, and recently separated from the army in the summer of 2020. He earned a Bronze Star, Combat and Expert Infantryman's Badges, Ranger Tab, and multiple other awards during his time in service.

Adam is passionate about incorporating all domains of health and fitness into programs for himself and the athletes he coaches. The optimal health journey achieves lifestyle shifts in nutrition, sleep, cognition, sociology, and training. Adam's goal is to combine his experience, education, and certifications to influence the tactical community of military, police, and fire services to succeed in addressing these health components.

For inquiries regarding coaching, podcast interviews, or public speaking, please reach out.

Email: whisleradam@gmail.com
Website: www.ttsprograms.com
LinkedIn: https://www.linkedin.com/in/adam-whisler-2021/

CHAPTER TWENTY-FIVE
NO CONCEPT OF FAILURE

By Doron Willis, LMFT, MA
Sports and Mental Performance Coach
Los Angeles, California

The difference between average people and achieving
people is their perception and response to failure.
—John Maxwell

How to perform at an optimal level in both sports and life has been studied for several years with many of the conclusions simply stating that an individual needs to be mentally tough. As true as this may be, many people do not quite understand the concept of mental toughness and the beliefs that help to cultivate such a trait. I credit my mother for instilling in me, at a very early age, the mindset of "no concept of F.A.I.L.U.R.E."

When I was eight years old, I had just finished playing my first season of Pop Warner football where my team went zero and six. After the season, I remember telling my mother that I did not know if I wanted to play the next season because the boys would be older and much bigger. Without missing a beat, my mother quickly turned to me and said, "They can't hit what they can't catch. All you have to do is keep finding ways to get better. When there is a will, there is a way." Needless to say, my speed was my biggest asset. It was in that moment my desire for success in sports and life was born. More importantly, I came to understand that it was okay to have fear, as long as I did not give in to it without first exhausting all of my resources to overcome that fear. Not surprisingly, this would not be the last time that I would experience a similar fear, not only in sports, but in life as well.

Just in case you are wondering, my Pop Warner team won the championship the following season, which I still feel was the best season of my athletic career even over getting a scholarship to play Division I college football and even after having been a state champion as a sprinter in high school.

So, what is failure? Failure has been defined by many terms such as the opposite of success, giving in, and the most popular one of them all, giving up. After many bouts with the trials and tribulations of life, I have come to define failure as an acronym. My acronym for failure is **F**earing **A**dversity **I**nstead of **L**earning to **U**tilize **R**esources **E**ffectively. Please allow me to inform you, if you have not discovered it already, but each level of your life that you aspire to ascend to, whether you are an athlete, business executive, or an entrepreneur, will present you with new challenges to test your willingness to rise up and overcome. I am willing to bet that the majority of successful people that we admire or see being showcased in our daily lives are individuals who have experienced fear, but courageously looked fear in the eyes and said, "Get the hell out of my way, I got goals to achieve and a purpose to fulfill!"

This brings me back to the summer going into my freshman year of high school. I was a 14-year-old one-hundred-and-fourteen-pound confident kid whose dreams of making it to the NFL were still in sight. My fear of trying out for the ninth-grade football team was very minimal due to the accomplishments that I had on the Pop Warner and middle school levels. I mean, after all I did to become a starter over an eighth grader when I was a seventh grader, what was there to be afraid of?

After having what I thought was a successful three-day try-out, I was both shocked and hurt when I did not see my name on the final list of players that made the team. I cried like a baby who wanted to be quickly changed out of a poopy diaper. In an instant, my dreams to continue playing the game I loved so much came to a screeching halt. I was on the verge of accepting someone's else's perception of not only my size, but my ability to do something that I knew I was quite skilled at. Thankfully, I had a community of support ranging from my family, former coaches, and peers who advocated on my behalf for the coach to give me a second chance. I will admit that I was super nervous when granted another opportunity to show that my size did not matter, but my past successes from playing overshadowed that fear. Long story short, I made the team. I scored the first touchdown of the season and played eight positions throughout the season. The coach would later apologize to me for prejudging my ability to play based on my size.

Some of the most successful athletes who have put their pride to side and received help in order to elevate their game include Kobe Bryant reaching out to his idol Michael Jordan; soccer star Alex Morgan working with legend Abby Wambach; Sidney Crosby being mentored by Mario Lemieux; and Lebron James seeking insights from legendary Duke University coach Mike Krzyzewski. If you have not figured it out by now, even the ones that we consider to be the greatest of all time needed help at some point during the course of their career. However, what stands out to me about these individuals is that they did not make failure an option. Hall of fame quarterback Peyton Manning once stated, "It's not wanting to win that makes you a winner; it's refusing to fail." Serena Williams even went as far as to say, "If you know anything about me, I hate to lose. I've always said I hate losing more than I like winning, so that drives me to be the best that I can be." It has been stated on several occasions that when you know your why, you will find a how.

In the end, I did not achieve my dream of playing in the NFL although I did have a few tryouts with the CFL and the Arena Football League. What I did not previously share were my reasons for wanting to play in the NFL. The reasons I wanted to be a professional football player was (1) to say that I played at the highest level; (2) to be able to boost my popularity (I mean, come on, I was a 22-year-old athlete full of ego); and (3), so that I could provide for my family and begin establishing generational wealth. My vision of the lifestyle that I wanted to create for me and my family was the source that motivated me to keep going.

Having a clear-cut vision is incredibly important when it comes to preventing failure from taking root in your psyche. As Helen Keller once eloquently stated, "The only thing worse than being blind is having sight but no vision." Oftentimes when we are faced with adversity, our brain has the tendency to ruminate on the negative event and keep us in this place known as the negativity bias. According to research, the negativity bias causes us to attach more strongly to trauma or rejection than to any kind of positive acknowledgement.

Two of my go-to methods to help me stay out of the negativity bias for an extended period of time are fact-checking my irrational thoughts and remembering my past successes. During moments of setback and perceived failure, the mind seems to somehow forget all of the positive qualities and inner strengths we possess that have helped us overcome previous challenges.

For example, when I was in my freshman year in college, I was not receiving any playing time due to a number of mental mistakes, which stemmed from performance anxiety. Slowly but surely, thoughts of doubt started to creep in about my ability to play at the collegiate level, and I found myself dreading wanting to even go to practice because of my fear of dropping a pass. Knowing that my poor performance was not because of my physical ability, but more so because of my mental state, I began to counter my irrational thoughts by implementing positive self-talk to reprogram my subconscious beliefs. For instance, I'd repeat, "I am gifted, talented, and capable." I also went back and watched old games from the past that reminded me of my capability. In doing this, I was able to regain my composure and decrease my fear of making a mistake, which earned me playing time as a true freshman.

In *Atomic Habits*, author James Clear states that failure happens in three phases. The failure of tactics, the failure of strategy, and the failure of vision. Clear shares that during the failure of tactics phase, individuals fail to implement effective tactics to help them achieve their desired goals. An athlete who has a mindset that has no concept of failure will always find a way to adjust their approach or tactic in order to execute a skill effectively. Elite athletes and individuals who have attained success at the highest level in their respective fields understand that regularly adjusting tactics is necessary to continue ascending to new levels of success.

The second reason that individuals allow failure to begin cultivating in their mind, according to James Clear, is the failure of strategy. Testing your strategy early and often will give you feedback and insight into what is or is not working. The reason why a lot of individuals fail to reach their desired goals is because of one of two reasons as it pertains to strategy: they are either (1) afraid to put their strategy to the test or (2) resistant to revamping their approach toward their goal. An athlete who spends all their time in the gym getting bigger, stronger, and faster, but is afraid to put it to the test in real time is unlikely to know if all their hard work is efficient. Additionally, an athlete who does put their hard work to the test but refuses to modify their strategy when they do not get the outcome they envisioned is essentially planning to fail.

The failure of vision is what prevents those seeking to be known as the best from reaching that top performance place. Essentially, they've failed to identify their why. Rosabeth Moss Kanter once shared that a vision is more than just a picture of what could be, but it is an appeal to become a better version of ourselves and a call to be more than what we currently are. I do not know any successful athlete or Fortune 500 CEO that did not have a vision before and during their quest for greatness. As mentioned previously, having a vision is key to combating the failure demons as it will be the fuel behind your efforts. Holding on to my vision of wanting to live a fulfilled life, create generational wealth, and make positive contributions to the world is what has kept me motivated and open to being flexible with my strategy and my tactics. More importantly, this has prevented me from giving in to adversity and giving up.

Back in 2006, I was having a difficult time establishing a flow for my life after sports, so I moved three thousand miles to Los Angeles with only five hundred dollars and a dream of winning an Oscar for best actor. Little did I know, life had different plans. While in pursuit of my dreams, life seemed to turn up the heat on the evolution of my soul's purpose and also my mindset. I got divorced after five years of marriage, which led me to question my existence, my purpose, and where my life was going. For a brief moment, I found myself contemplating packing up and moving back home where I would not have to worry as much about how I would sustain my life. However, the thought of doing that made me feel like I was giving up and adopting the mindset of a failure. So, I was able to redirect my thoughts back to my vision and tap into my ability to be resourceful. During this transition I not only went back to school to complete my undergraduate degree, but continued on to get my masters in clinical psychology with a concentration in marriage and family therapy. (Yes, the irony.)

While also in this phase of my transformation, I decided to challenge my mindset even more by participating in a ten-day silent meditation retreat. If you have never done a silent meditation retreat, not only is there no talking, but any form of entertainment is prohibited, so no reading, listening to music, working out, or writing. And to top it off, your car keys are confiscated. Being able to complete this retreat confirmed that I could achieve just about anything if I put my mind to it, which is typically the mindset of elite athletes and individuals of great success.

Through the many challenges that I have endured, I have come to realize like many people, that I fear failure. However, unlike most individuals' perspectives on the fear of failure, which usually consists of being afraid of making mistakes, I do not have that fear. My fear of failure revolves around me not getting back up and continuing on towards my purpose. I fear not living up to my potential regardless of how many setbacks or mistakes I endure along the way because each adverse moment is an opportunity to recalibrate and begin again.

I treat perceived failures like a chemistry experiment. Each time a specific strategy or tactic does not produce the outcome that I am seeking, I simply tell myself that I have successfully discovered what does not work and that I can eliminate that approach. This is similar to what Thomas Edison meant when he stated, "I have not failed. I've just found ten thousand ways that won't work." I will admit that going back to the drawing board can be annoying, but as I mentioned before, the fear of not maximizing my ability is what gets me back on my feet to keep going and prevents failure from living rent-free in my head.

I hope I have not misled you into believing that individuals who have achieved great success do not experience fear or doubts because they do. They just learn how to replace their fears with faith, and their doubts with relentless determination and grit. Even the late great Kobe Bryant once admitted to having fears and doubts, saying:

> I have self-doubts. I have insecurity. I have fear of failure. I have nights when I show up at the arena and I'm like, my back hurts, my feet hurts, my knees hurt. I don't have it. I just want to chill. We all have self-doubt. You don't deny it, but you also don't capitulate to it. You embrace it.

To sum it up, in order to experience success of any kind, especially the kind of success that will get you labeled as elite, great, or a genius, then you have to develop a mindset that cannot conceptualize failure. To recap, you must:

First, establish your vision, or your why, as this will be the wind beneath your sail when the waters get a little rocky. Or the fuel to your tank when it is running close to empty. Make sure it is something that is greater than just meeting your needs, but also your vision should be one that could possibly benefit others as serving a greater good can oftentimes propel us forward.

Second, know that having fears and doubts is normal. However, successful people do not give in to these fears and doubts by dwelling on the worst things that can happen, but instead they focus on the best possible outcome. This also goes back to that old saying, "If your dreams don't scare you, then they are not big enough." The next time you are experiencing butterflies while in pursuit of your dreams, remind yourself that this is normal, and then begin starving your fears and doubts by feeding your faith and courage through intentional action.

Third, do not be rigid in your approach. As I pointed out earlier in this chapter, you have to be flexible and willing to readjust your game plan.

Remember, treat every setback as a chemistry experiment that has successfully helped you pinpoint the things that do and do not work. Do not forget the letters U, R, and E, in my acronym for failure—Utilize Resources Effectively. In essence this means, do not be afraid to modify if you have to.

Fourth, to piggyback off of the third point, you have to see perceived failures as an opportunity to begin again, but this time more wisely. Those who we have achieved the success that we desire typically see an opportunity in every moment of adversity. And their mindset and self-talk is usually, "If not me, then who?" Being optimistic does not mean you are naive or blind to the problem; it's just that you are not focused on the problem. You are focused on the opportunity of the things that can be.

When met with a challenge, it is okay to take a step back to vent and express your frustrations, but give yourself a time limit to do so and then get right back to it. Failure is not a word, phrase, or thought in the minds of those who are considered elite athletes or genius innovators. They will exhaust every possible resource readily available to them because they know that fear and doubt are just illusions in the mind.

About the Author

Doron Willis is a former collegiate football player and fitness trainer turned psychotherapist (LMFT). Throughout the course of his journey, Doron quickly learned that in order for him to be successful, he had to develop a mindset that had no concept of failure despite the setbacks. Doron's mindset was cultivated through many life experiences such as getting cut from the ninth-grade football team, failing out of college, going through a divorce, and enduring financial hardships. These challenges ended up helping Doron become conscious of how to thrive through hardship.

Doron's primary goal is to assist individuals with establishing a resilient mindset that will help them maximize their potential and perform in life at an optimal level, especially athletes. Doron is a NAMA Certified Anger Management Specialist-II, trained in EMDR therapy, holds a Sports & Exercise Psychology certificate, and is a Performance Enhancement Specialist. Doron's philosophy is: setbacks are inevitable, but failure is an option.

To learn more about Doron, visit www.doronwillis.com

PERFORMANCE MINDSET

By Jack Seversen
Student Athlete
Los Angeles, California

Whether you think you can or think you can't, you're right.
—Henry Ford

This quote from Henry Ford helped change my perspective on the limits of what is possible. It instigated in me the realization that physical and mental limits are created in the mind.

In the spring of my freshman year of high school, I was introduced to the sport of track and field. I had run cross country in middle school, so I was no stranger to running, but I was a stranger to the soft, red running surface of the track. Even at the start of the track season, I had a great group of friends to train with. Most of them were my buddies from elementary and middle school, and we all entered into this new sport with an excited attitude. The distance coach on the team, Coach Mar, was also excited to have us on the team. During that year Coach Mar trained us, we worked hard, and we all got to the mid-five-minutes in the 1600 meters, which is about ten steps (30 feet) shorter than a mile. By the middle of my freshman year of track, I achieved a time of 5:11 in the 1600 meter, and I was very proud. I was motivated to break five minutes before the season ended, but I didn't quite do it.

My sophomore year of track eventually came, and I was not putting up the same times as I was in my freshman year. I wasn't happy. My best mile time of my sophomore year was about 5:30, so my sub-five-minute mile seemed far out of reach.

Junior year track and field season came quickly, and I felt ready. After a good cross-country season in the fall and a restful winter, I felt prepared for a great track season. My baseline 1600-meter time in practice was about 5:25. It wasn't great, but for practice, it wasn't terrible. One of the most misunderstood components of running is the impact of adrenaline. In a practice, it's hard to perform to the same caliber as a competition because of the lack of adrenaline. It's interesting, though, because in martial arts, football, and many other physical sports, we more often think of the impact of adrenaline, but in running, nobody I was around really talked about it. I made this realization at the start of my junior year, and from then on, I tried to train by mimicking the stress of a meet. I've always been competitive to beat both rival competitors and teammates, but at this point, I wanted to beat myself as well.

Once the first track meet arrived, I achieved a time of 5:15. I was excited to be getting closer to my personal best of 5:11. I talked to Coach Mar about my goal of breaking the five-minute mile. I trained the hardest I had ever trained. Every day was a race day, every day felt real as I visualized running in competition. I was excited for Saturday's meet because I felt like I had improved a lot even with only one solid week of training.

Saturday morning came, and I was pumped. I was trying to prepare as much as possible, really hoping I would cut 15 seconds and break five minutes, or at least run a personal best. As I trained, I didn't really tell anybody about my goals. I didn't want to encounter any unnecessary expectations from the outside, so I kept my goals to myself. Finally, the time came.

With my heart beating heavily, my breathing calm, and my toe one inch from the starting line, the starting gun shot! I sprinted out rapidly for a good position. I remember my teammates on the sideline cheering me on, and it encouraged me to run faster. As I watched my splits, I noticed that I was not on pace to break five minutes, but it didn't slow me down. As I started the last lap, I shifted my mindset to breaking my record of 5:11. As I finished, I achieved the time of 5:17.

This race was a big disappointment for me. Everything had felt so good, but I got two seconds slower than I had the prior week. How was this possible—I'd trained harder, prepared better, but had run slower.

I became very discouraged after this race, but it didn't stop me from training hard. I continued to train throughout the week, but I needed to change something. That week I put up similar times to my baseline in practice. Then something shifted.

It was during this time that I stumbled across the Henry Ford quote: "Whether you think you can or think you can't, you're right." This quote is saying that if you think you can do something, you're right, and you will do it. It is also saying, if you don't think you can do something, you're right, and you can't. My entire mindset changed immediately after I heard this quote, and I started rethinking the way I run. I started truly *thinking* that my running would improve, believing it would improve, not hoping that it would improve.

The following Saturday, after another intense week of training, we had our next meet. This time it was different. I still prepared similarly to how I had before, but this time I knew I was going to break the five-minute 1600. I had the training and the fitness; I just needed a switch in mindset. With this new mindset, I started focusing on my breathing before my race. I lay on the ground, closed my eyes, and breathed heavily in a meditation-like manner. I pictured what I was about to do, which was breaking five minutes in the 1600 meter. As I was warming up, I was telling everyone that this was the day. I was so pumped up, telling everyone to watch me finally break my goal. I knew today would be the day.

I stepped up to the starting line, picturing the whole race in my head, the whole strategy I knew I would execute. The starting pistol shot, and I was off! I was running a varsity race, and the adrenaline was pumping through my body as we started faster than I was used to. After the first lap, I started settling into my pace, maintaining a strong, yet doable run. As I crossed the 800-meter mark, I saw that my time was about 2:25, which was on pace to break the five-minute mile limit. The third lap is when most runners really feel the pain. Successful runners have to keep pushing through the pain.

As I rounded the third lap, my split was looking good. Needing to run a fast 400 meters, I picked up my pace, and I started my kick with 200 meters left. I started giving the rest I had, leaving it all on the track. As I rounded the last corner to the straight away, my eyes shifted to the clock. It read 4:35. I focused on my last 100 meters. I didn't care about anyone else but myself running this race. It was going to be close. As the clock ticked up towards five minutes, I gave everything I had. I crossed the finish line with a time of 4:58.

As I crossed the finish line and went to the side, I was overwhelmed with cheers and support from my teammates and coaches. I was ecstatic to finally have reached this goal. As I cooled down, I thought about my race and how

I had prepared for it. Why did I reach this goal? Why did I shave almost 20 seconds off of my time from last week? Meditation with purposeful breathing probably helped, but the quote I had heard popped back into my head. "Whether you think you can or think you can't, you're right." I knew I could break the sub-five-minute 1600 on that today, and I did. I knew I was going to break five minutes before my race even started, and that's what I did. I had a new mindset, which changed my view on running and everything else as well.

Just hearing the quote made me think about how strong the mind is, and my mind told my body to ignore its limitations. But then another thought entered my mind: "Was this just a fluke?" I was still overly excited, looking at my official time throughout the day, but I was curious if I could run this time again the following week, and the weeks after that.

In the Monday practice after I had accomplished my goal, I felt like I was the person to beat in the mile. There was a target on me, so I trained harder that week, and my teammates did too. That week, after solid practice and recovery, I was ready for another meet. Going into this meet, I was a bit nervous about how I would do. I didn't want the past race to just be a fluke. I didn't want the hype and excitement that my teammates had for me to fade away. This was a bit of a dangerous mindset to have, so I tuned it all out and focused on myself and what I *knew* I could do. I had already proven that it was possible for me to run sub-five minutes. I literally knew it was possible, and now it was about to be done again.

I wanted to prepare the exact same way as I'd done for the previous race. That included meditating, my warm up, and eating a sausage egg McMuffin hours before the race. I felt great throughout the morning, and when the race came, I was locked in. That race, I achieved a time of 4:52. I couldn't believe that I shaved six seconds off of my personal best from the previous week. In addition, 25 seconds from my time two weeks prior. This proved that my first sub-five wasn't a fluke and that I had made a true breakthrough because of a simple change in my mindset.

I was stoked, and it honestly surprised me and my coaches how much I improved my times during those weeks. With two meets left, I made a new goal of breaking 4:50. It's not greed that prompted me to create this new goal, for I was already happy about my times, but it was so I had a reason and drive to keep running hard. The next week, I did everything the same as before in preparation, except for one thing—I woke up a bit late that morning and didn't have time to go buy a sausage egg McMuffin. Physically I was ready, but mentally I was not there. I told myself, "You will break 4:50 today," but I'm not totally sure that I believed it. I ran the race, and finished with a time of 4:53, which was one second slower than the prior week. I believe that I didn't reach my goal because even though I told myself that I would run fast, a small piece of my mind didn't believe it because I was fixated on the idea that my routine had changed.

I wasn't necessarily disappointed in my time because I still was so thankful that I was even running at this level, but it did motivate me for the final race the following week. Going into the final race, I knew I had to prepare like usual, but also, I knew I had to go into it with a new meaning. I really wanted to run this race, not only for myself, but also for my coaches. They had helped me so much throughout the year and always believed in me. I didn't want this to distract me from the race, but it made me want to make them happy and proud for the last race. I remember in my warmups, like I did before, I told everyone to watch me run sub 4:50. I knew that I was going to do this. I also thoroughly remember telling my coaches to make sure they were watching (I knew they would be anyway) because I was going to break 4:50. I was hyped up and physically and mentally ready.

As I got my number and pinned it to my jersey, I breathed slowly as I prepared for this last race of the season. I stepped up to the starting line and patiently waited for the start to get set up. As I waited, I visualized success. This was it. "You've been training for this moment the whole season," I said to myself. "Everything you've worked for, and have in you, needs to be put down now."

I looked up and got set as the starting gun was raised. Then we were off!

I went out fast, eventually finding my pace. I was in an extremely fast varsity race. I kept in my groove running my race, and pushed through the third lap as the pain started settling into my legs. As I started my last lap, I saw that my pace was better than ever by a second or two. I really had to push it on this last lap. As I rounded the first corner of the lap, I saw Coach Jackson, and he was screaming at me to keep running strong. This was it. "Mind over matter" is easy to say, but hard to perform as the lactic acid builds up in your legs, and every part of your body is telling you to stop and fall down.

As I rounded the last corner, I saw Coach Mar. He yelled for me to finish strong. I thought about how this would be the last 100 meters Coach Mar would ever see me run, so I had to give it all for him. As I sprinted the final stretch, I wasn't sure I'd make it in time to break 4:50. I knew it was going to be close as I pushed through every painful movement and thought that was telling me to slow down. My mind was pushing my body to do what I knew it could do. Fifty meters, 40 meters, 30 meters. The clock was getting dangerously close to 4:50. Twenty meters, 10 meters, FINISH!

As I crossed the finish line, I ran and fell onto the football field in the center of the track. I knew it was close, and my mind did all it could to make me doubt my results. As I waited for the official time to show up on the big scoreboard of the stadium, Coach Mar and my teammates ran to me to give me water and congratulate me on a good race.

I waited, and eventually the time was posted. It was 4:49.81 seconds. I was absolutely overwhelmed with congratulations from my teammates and coaches. I was so excited and proud to have done what I told them and told myself that I could do.

That track and field season taught me a lot. Of course, I learned how important training was and why we need to eat healthily and recover, but I also learned about other things like how meaningful support is when reaching our goals. I definitely couldn't have done this without the help and support of my coaches and teammates. The main lesson I learned during that season was the importance of mindset. The mind has way more control over our physical abilities than most people think. For me, the mindset shift was from hoping I would reach my goal to knowing I would reach my goal. If we can trick our mind into knowing it will do something, we have no limits as long as we truly believe it. As Henry Ford once said, "Whether you think you can or think you can't, you're right."

About the Author

Jack Seversen is a senior at Wiseburn Da Vinci Science High School in Los Angeles, California. With a can-do mindset, Jack is always striving to reach new goals. Some of the goals Jack has completed include running a sub-five-minute mile, completing a full Ironman (2.4-mile swim, 112-mile bike, 26.2-mile run), and climbing the highest mountains in Nevada, Arizona, and Colorado's Mt. Elbert (highest mountain in the Rockies). Jack runs cross country and track for his high school, and he enjoys playing the guitar, skiing, and surfing. Jack's goals are to continue to learn about himself through adventures in nature and to continue to learn about people through relationships with his friends, family, church, and school groups.

Email: jqseversen@gmail.com

DID YOU ENJOY THIS BOOK?

If you enjoyed reading this book, you can help by suggesting it to someone else you think might like it, and **please leave a positive review** wherever you purchased it. This does a lot in helping others find the book. We thank you in advance for taking a few moments to do this.

THANK YOU

If you enjoyed reading this book, don't miss the other books in the Peak Performance Series:

Peak Performance: Mindset Tools for Business

Peak Performance: Mindset Tools for Entrepreneurs

Peak Performance: Mindset Tools for Leaders

You might also like other Thin Leaf Press titles:

Winning Mindset: Elite Strategies for Peak Performance

Winner's Mindset: Peak Performance Strategies for Success

The Successful Mind: Tools to Living a Purposeful, Productive, and Happy Life

The Successful Body: Using Fitness, Nutrition, and Mindset to Live Better

The Successful Spirit: Top Performers Share Secrets to a Winning Mindset

Made in the USA
Las Vegas, NV
11 March 2024

87074459R00125